ON THE EDGE

Personal Flying Experiences
During the Second World War

by Robert G. Brown

Foreword by Norman C. Brown

Published by

 GENERAL STORE
PUBLISHING HOUSE

1 Main Street Brunstown, Ontario, Canada K0J 1G0
Telephone (613) 432-7697 or 1-800-465-6072

ISBN 1-896182-87-9
Printed and bound in Canada

Canadian Cataloguing in Publication Data

Brown, Robert G.
   On the edge: personal flying experiences during the Second World War

ISBN 1-896182-87-9

1. Brown, Robert G. 2. World War, 1939-1945 – Aerial operations,
British. 3. World War, 1939-1945 – Personal narratives, Canadian. 4.
Great Britain. Royal Air Force – Biography. I. Title.

D786.B76 1998   940.54'4941'092   C98-900332-9

First Printing 1999

Acknowledgements

※

My Daughter-In-Law, Joanne, who did most of the original typing and initiated the dividing of this long narrative into more easily read chapters.

※

My Son, George, who by continually pointing out the "on-the-edge" character of the daily incidents both in the air and later on the ground, effectively provided the "ON-THE -EDGE" title.

Dedication

These recollections are dedicated to:

<u>*My Wife,*</u>
*who must have wondered what on earth I was doing over there
so long, while she tended war casualties over here in the
Canadian Women's Army Corps Hospital.*

<u>*My Father,*</u>
*for whom I really wish I had completed these writings
while he was alive.*

<u>*My Brother,*</u>
who, in far off India, flew against an even more ruthless enemy.

<u>*My Sons,*</u>
*who, I hope, will gain something from my experiences which
will help them in their own lives.*

Contents

FOREWORD

It is a pleasure and an honour to be asked to write these few words to acknowledge the efforts of "one of ours" who in the field of flying and during a really bad war, made that war his personal challenge and from enlistment was prepared to do his best to help win it—albeit in his own way.

My brother, Rob, was different than most in that despite all the confusion and haste of those early days he managed to choose the type of war job he wanted to do and the perfect tool, the perfect aircraft, to do it with.

Most of us just flew whatever aircraft the R.A.F had available. We didn't much care what the job was, provided it was exciting and that there was a fair chance of getting back—preferably in one piece.

The role he chose was "fighters" and the aircraft was the North American P51 Mustang—probably the best long range fighter aircraft of the second world war. Fast, agile and unforgiving, it was a formidable weapon in the hands of the right pilot.

This then is the story of one such pilot. A pilot so dedicated and determined that he continually pushed his wonderful machine to the very edge and beyond to best serve his cause and his country.

In the game of war the stakes are high and so regretfully it comes as no surprise that "Lady Luck" blinked one fateful night and he found himself descending by parachute into an unfriendly place, where the Gestapo and other unsavoury types ruled supreme.

F/L Robert G. Brown was reported missing, June 18th, 1944. Some time later the bad news filtered through to India where I was serving with the R.A.F. in South East Asia Command. With the war better than half over, it was a devastating blow to me and I knew equally so to his wife and our families back in Canada. However, having spent most of my formative years with Rob in the rural, even primitive setting of the Toronto Island, fishing, boating, ice boating and even walking across the frozen bay to school, I knew him to be hard to beat. I really felt that he would probably make it back despite all odds.

Suffice to say that many a "Burra Peg" were downed in relief and joy when the good news "Safe & Well" finally came through.

I warmly commend this book to you. Not because he wrote it but rather because it is a fascinating and intimate peek into a fighter pilot's personal experiences and thoughts during a quite terrible war.

Norman C. Brown DFC CD

Major General (Ret'd)

x

1. Disarmament, Appeasement and Apathy: The Path to War

Following the end of the First World War, the mistaken idea that disarmament of all countries would prevent war in the future took hold. The military forces of the victorious countries were allowed to deteriorate during the 1920s and the 1930s, continuing even after 1933, when Adolf Hitler became chancellor of Germany, and proceeded to build up his country's forces completely against the restrictions of the Versailles Treaty.

Hitler could have been stopped early in his career, but the Allied countries were too weak, both in armaments and in resolve, so that nothing was done to enforce the terms of the treaty. I was just a young man, barely out of my teens, but I remember wondering how the world could stand by while both Germany and Italy provided troops and equipment to enable Franco to defeat the loyalist forces to become dictator of Spain. Except for a few hundred, mostly American volunteers, no one helped Spain to remain democratic.

Shortly after bringing his forces out of Spain, Hitler marched into Austria, and then into Czechoslovakia. The world was finally concerned, but far too weak to do anything but protest verbally. Germany's armed forces, after their operational training, during the Spanish Civil War, were now formidable, and obviously the best in the world. High profile people like Charles Lindbergh, and U.S. ambassador to the U.K., Joe Kennedy, did everything they could to convince the Allies to stay out of any conflict. These so-called-leaders believed that we could not win.

At this time Hitler invited the world's leaders to meet him in Munich, Germany, where he assured them that he had no further plans to attack any country. Prime Minister Neville Chamberlain of Britain attended and later when he returned home, stood up in the

House of Commons to announce that he thought that "Hitler was rather a nice chap, really," and predicted, "Peace in our time."

Within the week Hitler unleashed a mammoth air and ground attack against Poland—so much for peace. As a result, Britain declared war on Germany on September 3, 1939, followed seven days later by Canada and the war was on. Chamberlain resigned and Winston Churchill became Prime Minister, promising the country not a fantasy peace based on surrender, but blood, sweat and tears to finally win against the enemy. Hitler was busy for the next few weeks flattening Warsaw, so nothing much happened in the west, and the period was dubbed "The Phoney War."

The British Expeditionary Force moved into France behind the French Maginot Line, a modernized First World War-style line of trenches running along the entire border with Germany. The Germans had built a similar trench defence line on their border, called the Siegfried Line.

In the First World War, when Allied generals planned an attack, it began with a massive artillery bombardment of the enemy trench line, which would be lifted to allow thousands of our infantry to climb out of the trenches and "go-over-the-top" with their rifles and fixed bayonets. They would charge across the no-man's-land between the trenches and attempt to capture the enemy trenches. The enemy soldiers simply kept their heads down during the bombardment, and then, still protected by their trenches, were able to mow down the attacking troops with their rifle and machine gun fire. The troops charging at them were completely exposed. No one thought of utilizing body armour, to protect against the flying bullets, or even have them push protective shields ahead of them, as they did in earlier days, to protect against spears and arrows. Although the machine guns could fire at the rate of 600 rounds per minute, and they, of course, did not have bullet-proof materials in those days, any protection would have saved thousands of lives.

All during the war, both sides utilized these unprotected "over-the-top" attacks. It cost hundreds of thousands of lives for really no lasting territory gain. The Allies were expecting the same kind of a war this time, but Hitler, when he had finished with Poland, mounted a massive attack, not against the front of the Maginot Line, but around the right flank through Belgium, where he encountered little or no opposition. He then swung left and attacked the rear of the Maginot Line and France was out of the war. The British Forces had to flee to England via the Dunkirk beaches, following the collapse of the French armies, and suffered tremendous losses.

Hitler utilized the "fifth column," in France and the other countries in Europe to so weaken them that their defeat was made quick and certain. Armies marched into battle in four columns of men. The "fifth column" of secret spying and corruption performed before the battle, accomplished, it was estimated, at least that equal to having a fifth column of fighting soldiers on the battle field.

Over the years Hitler had sent his spies to infiltrate the European countries to such an extent that when Germany finally attacked, there was almost no opposition.

In Norway, Prime Minister Quisling was such a traitor, welcoming the enemy troops with open arms when they came across his border, that his name now means "traitor," and is so defined in the Oxford Dictionary.

Great Britain now stood alone, her only defence against the coming massive enemy attack and invasion was the Royal Air Force and the natural barrier of the English Channel.

2. Pilot Training

I joined the Royal Canadian Air Force in late 1940. I had just completed a thirty-day stint in the Queen's Own Rifles at Camp Borden. We spent the time drilling on the Parade Square, going on long route marches, doing bayonet practice on straw-filled dummies and some rifle firing, none of which was of much interest to me. I was called up by the air force, but had to await the assessment of my medical examination. I was applying for aircrew, where the physical requirements were higher than normal. My E.E.G. had shown that rather than having one signal from my brain to my heart per heartbeat, I had two signals, or voltage pulses. This made for a rather weird E.E.G. trace, however my heart never missed a beat and the doctors finally cleared me for aircrew. *In 1967 when I was in Churchill, Manitoba at the National Research Council Rocket Range, and had to spend a few days in hospital, the doctors took an E.E.G. and they too were very concerned. They sent the records down to Winnipeg for study, but eventually advised me that although it was unusual, it wasn't a defect.*

I reported to the R.C.A.F. Manning Pool at the Canadian National Exhibition in Toronto, Ontario, and walked right into an epidemic of scarlet fever. We were housed in the automotive building and given "pap" tests to see whether or not we tested positive for the disease. Those whose tests were positive were to be quarantined. I tested positive and although I never did catch the disease, I was a carrier. We were sleeping in double-decker steel beds. I slept in a lower bed and practically every night for the next three weeks, I would be awakened by the medical people carrying the occupant of the upper bed off to the hospital. Twice a day we had to climb the stairs to the mezzanine for temperature parade. I used to be very careful to walk slowly so that my temperature wouldn't go up—I did not want to go to hospital. This of course had nothing to do with body temperature. The doctors were just looking for signs of infection. I never had a temperature. Those that were healthy like me, went on daily ten-mile-route marches all around Toronto to keep in shape.

After about three weeks in quarantine, I was posted for basic guard duty to Dartmouth, Nova Scotia, across the harbour from Halifax. We were to guard the R.C.A.F. Shearwater seaplane base, where a squadron of Super Marine Stranraer Flying Boats was engaged in escorting troop transport convoys and general anti-submarine duties in the sea lanes of the Atlantic Ocean.

We were on duty around the clock, two hours on and four hours off, marching up and down around the base perimeter in the snow and rain with our rifles over our shoulders, providing protection against the enemy, who, I was sure, was thousands of miles away.

One day I was talking to one of the Stranraer pilots and asked him if I could go with him on his next flight. He said that he was taking off in a few minutes and I would be welcome aboard. I thought that he would be going on a flight of an hour or so. We returned to base almost four hours later, and although I enjoyed looking down on the troop and naval ships that escorted them, it was a long flight, and the Stranraer was a pretty old aeroplane, not even a washroom on board. I was glad to get back, and just made it in time to do my guard duty shift. The sergeant probably wondered why I was breathing so hard, having run the last few hundred yards, but I just grabbed my rifle and headed out in the rain to protect the base against the "bad guys." Actually, a few enemy submarines were spotted off-shore in the St. Lawrence River mouth during the war, but I encountered no suspicious people on my watch. It was probably just as well, as I was given just two .303 bullets to bring down the spies.

After three weeks or so, I was posted to Victoriaville, Quebec for (I.T.S.) Initial Training School to learn the theory of flight, meteorology, navigation and other subjects to do with flying. The town was almost completely French-speaking, but we were not particularly affected as we were too busy studying. We attended classes until quite late in the evening. To keep in shape, I had to run late at night through the town park. It was very good exercise, but I kept tripping over the exposed tree roots which I couldn't see in the dark, so I managed to keep in good physical condition, but slightly black and blue.

After two weeks, I was given a day off. I travelled by bus to a nearby (E.F.T.S.) Elementary Flying Training School at Cap-de-la-Madeleine, Quebec, to see if I could get a flight in one of the Fleet Finch aeroplanes. I was concerned that although I was learning the theory of flying, and found it very interesting, I really knew nothing of the practical aspect. Other than one short flight in a small plane in the 1930s and the recent trip in the Stranraer, I had never really flown. Would I get airsick? Would I really like flying? Would I be any good? I hoped to get the answers once and for all by doing an hour of aerobatics in a Fleet Finch which was particularly good for all aerobatic manoeuvres.

I spoke to the chief flying instructor, who introduced me to one of his instructors, who he said would love to give me an hour's aerobatic workout. They gave me a parachute and I climbed into the aircraft with the instructor. He took off and climbed to about 10,000 feet and for the next hour we did everything in the book. We were upside down for at least half of the time. We did loops, rolls, rolls-off-the-top and stall turns by the dozens. The instructor was very good. He let me fly for a short time, but I was really just steering the aircraft, not really flying it. I found that the violent aerobatic manoeuvres in the clear blue sky were very exhilarating and enjoyable to me. When the hour was over and we came in to touch down on the runway again, I knew that flying was what I wanted to do and there would be nothing that I couldn't learn to handle. The only thing left to find out was, would I be good enough?

After Victoriaville, I was posted to the (E.F.T.S.) Elementary Flying in Oshawa, Ontario, where we flew Tiger Moths. The flying instructors were almost all ex-bush pilots who were not exactly kindly or orthodox in their teaching methods, but were nevertheless experts in the art of flying. My instructor, Sergeant Hogarth, used to shout a lot, but since the content of each message, shouted from the back seat, made so much sense, I simply ignored the volume level and learned.

The author after an aerobatic workout in the Fleet Finch. E.F.T.S., Cap-de-la-Madeleine, Quebec.

After soloing in the Tiger Moth, following six hours or so of dual instruction from the sergeant, I found that I had an above average aptitude for it. Had I not been able, I would have preferred to be washed-out, as many were. Flying was too demanding for average skills and far too dangerous, particularly in wartime even when enemy action is excluded.

About half-way through the course I was up for cross-country flying practice, so I thought that I would fly to Toronto and say, "Hi" to my father. My father was chief of the High Level pumping station for the City of Toronto waterworks. I flew the fifty miles or so to Toronto, followed along Bloor Street and then north at Avenue Road. I flew up Avenue Road to Rathnelly Street and right over the High Level station, and my father's house beside it. I looked down at the house and at the fish pond in the backyard. Although I flew around above the house for some time, I saw nothing of my father.

I would have liked to have flown low over the house, but flying regulations forbade flying below 2,000 feet. Low flying was a court-martial offence. You had to stay at, or above, 2,000 feet over built-up areas, so that in case of engine failure, you could glide out of the city and not mess up the downtown buildings by crashing into them. My father was obviously not at home, so I returned to Oshawa.

The first time I did a roll in the Tiger Moth for Sergeant Hogarth, he shouted from the rear cockpit, "What do you call that?" I advised that I thought that I had done a roll. "That was a barrel roll you did. I want a point roll where the nose of the aircraft never moves off a selected point on the horizon as the aircraft rotates the full 360°." I, of course, had to learn how to do it properly. Doing a barrel roll, although not a precision manoeuvre, is far more fun.

While executing the barrel roll, the aircraft travels hundreds of feet all round the sky, usually down, left, right and then back up, roughly following the circumference of a huge barrel. The air force though, insisted on the more precision version.

I didn't know until many months later that although flying a Mustang was much more difficult than flying a Tiger Moth, when performing aerobatics the reverse is true. Mainly because of the low engine power it is very difficult to keep the nose up. To do a roll in a Mustang required just a flick of the joystick, left, or right, with no rudder action required.

On the other hand, performing a point roll in a Tiger Moth with the nose of the aircraft staying exactly on a point on the horizon throughout, required a real workout. To do a left-hand point roll, the nose of the aircraft is first brought up to the horizon line by pulling back the stick. The joystick is then moved fully over to the left. This turns the aircraft over on its left side, so that the elevators now act as rudders, and must be quickly brought back to the neutral position to prevent the nose moving off the horizon point. The actual rudder, which is now horizontal, must be utilized as an elevator surface to keep the aircraft nose on the horizon. Usually full application of the right rudder pedal is required to prevent the nose from dropping.

As the aircraft rotates to the inverted position, the elevators are once again acting as elevators, but require the pushing forward of the stick to keep the nose up now, rather than pulling back and the rudder must be centralized! As the roll continues, the aircraft turns onto its right side and, once again, the rudder has to be used and the elevators centered, this time with full application of the left rudder pedal to prevent the nose dropping. When the aircraft completes the final ninety degrees of the roll and is returned to level flight, the aircraft's vertical control returns once again to the elevators. The rudder should be centered and the aircraft nose should be still on the horizon line.

Towards the end of the elementary flying course at Oshawa, I was up practising and sensed that there was something wrong. Then it hit me. I hadn't heard a word from the sergeant in the back seat for a long time. I had been doing take-off and landings for the last half-hour or so, which in the past had prompted a, "Do you call that a landing?" from him every time. I turned around quickly to see if he was sick or dead or something, but he seemed normal.

On my fifty-hour flying test performed for the visiting R.C.A.F. officer, I was given an above-average rating. I shook hands with Sergeant Hogarth before leaving Oshawa and thanked him for his patience. He was quite a different person now—almost happy.

I was posted to S.F.T.S. St. Hubert, Quebec, for Service Flying Training on Harvards. The Harvards had a Pratt and Whitney rotary, air-cooled engine, which made it much faster than the Tiger Moth. It had a tendency to ground-loop when landing and made a characteristic high-pitched whining sound when the propeller was in fine pitch.

It performed well otherwise, and Alec Ince and I, besides learning the flying skills on the course, also spent a fair amount of time on perfecting low flying, and head-on attacks, which not only were not on the course, but were forbidden. Because of a very understanding chief of flying, who luckily was an ex-Battle of Britain pilot and who probably had used these tactics many times himself, we were not washed out and our standing in the class did not seem to be harmed. He simply said that we were not to do that anymore. Actually it proved to be the most important part of my training, as I ended up on a squadron that did all of its operations at low level with very aggressive head-on attacks as the main defence.

E.F.T.S. Oshawa in Ontario was privately operated. The food provided to the student pilots, although not fancy, was very good, and very well prepared. At S.F.T.S. St. Hubert, the station was operated by the R.C.A.F. with food supplied by a local civilian contractor. Compared with that provided at Oshawa, the quality of the food and its preparation, dropped drastically. I certainly noticed the difference, but I felt that I was there to learn to fly, not eat well. As long as the food wasn't rotten and didn't affect my flying, I wasn't overly concerned. A number of other student pilots were really incensed to such an extent that they pretty well went on strike. It was so serious that Ottawa sent a senior officer down to settle the matter. We were advised that the officer would be visiting the base the next day and would sample the food for himself. The next day the dinner menu changed magically. Roast chicken with all the trimmings was served, and predictably the inspecting officer really relished asking us just why we would find fault with such excellent food! The next day, after the officer had returned to air force headquarters, the food returned to what could only be described as slop, and flying training continued.

Knowing the country as I do now, the local food supplier probably made huge profits on his contract, with some going to pay off the officer. The officer should have kept his visitation time secret, so that his inspection would have meant something. We were all very young, but we were not children.

The training program kept us very busy. We would fly in the morning, attend ground school in the afternoon and after dinner until as late as 11:30 p.m., we would do Link Trainer exercises which would complement our flying.

It was now early winter and the weather was not the best for flying in any case. One of the student pilots crashed and was killed one very foggy night. Because several students had ground-looped after touching down on the icy runway, crashing into the very high snow banks along the sides of the runway and extensively damaging the aircraft, it was announced that henceforth anyone ground-looping would be washed-out immediately. Although I had never ground-looped and had mastered my landing problems at Oshawa, I still was very apprehensive each time I came in to land!

Landing an aircraft is an unique skill, probably the most important and most difficult to learn. Many pilots didn't find landing a problem at all, at first and could three-point the aircraft on the runway every time, until they encountered cross winds, ice and snow on the runway, violent wind squalls, etc., when they would fail to take the proper action, and would end up ground-looping and damaging the aeroplanes.

In my case, Sergeant Hogarth at Oshawa had not been shouting for nothing. My landings were not good. In time though, and not too much time, as it had to be within the maximum of eight hours dual flying before soloing, I mastered the art and became almost expert at making good landings under the most hectic conditions, particularly in England where they seemed to insist on building all airfield runways so that cross-wind landings would always be required.

Most airfields in England employed three runways laid out to take advantage of the prevailing wind directions so that pilots would have the choice of using the runway which was more or less into wind. The problem was, though, that although under clear skies the wind could be straight down one of the runways, clear skies were few and far between in England, particularly during the winter months, and cross-winds were the norm. Because of the many storm squalls when the wind would continuously vary widely in both speed and direction, constant adjustment of landing tactics was required. The pilot would have to counter any sideway motion which could damage the undercarriage when the wheels touched, by either lowering a wing or doing a flat turn, or "crab," into the wind to equal the side wind force. At the last second or so of the

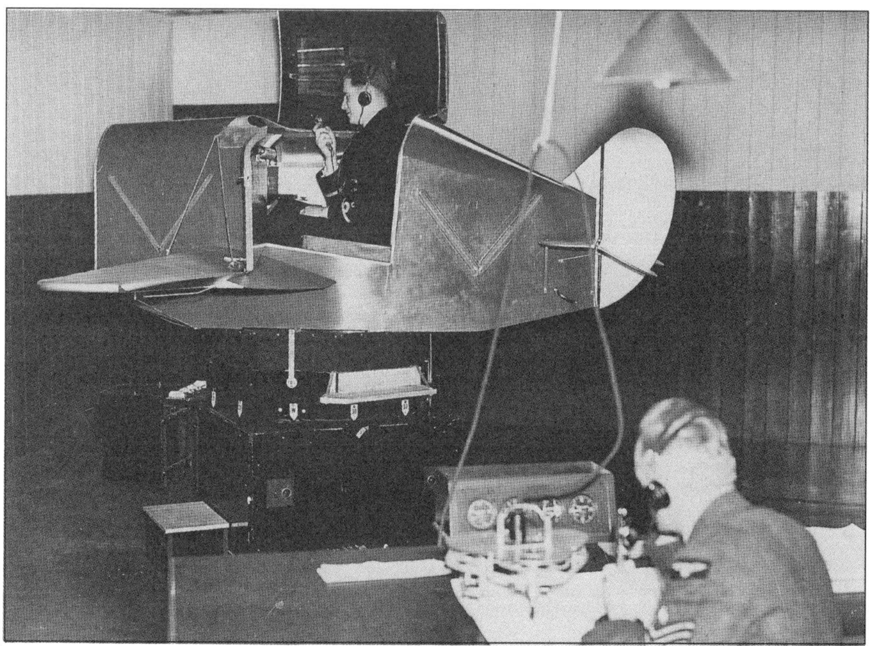

The Link Trainer. An effective and inexpensive means of complementing instrument flying for pilots.

Source: *An Illustrated History of the R.A.F.* ©1990 Colour Library Books Ltd., Keystone Collection

landing procedure, the pilot must quickly raise the lowered wing so that it does not strike the ground, or apply the rudder to remove the flat turn and fly straight in line with the runway so that a good landing results. I believe that I became good mainly because, in my learning process, I had to land from every weird position over the runway. When I later found myself being blown violently sideways and perhaps a wing being lifted by a storm squall at the last second before touching down on the runway, I was not unduly concerned and simply applied the proper corrective action as I had done countless times before. While at Oshawa, some of my bounces had put me in far worse positions over the runway and I had learned to get the aeroplane down safely, so this was no big deal.

When landing, the pilot has to observe the broad scene before him, comprised of the horizon line where the earth and sky appear to come together, the airfield and the runway upon which he is about to land. Once over the airfield boundary fence with wheels and flaps down and he is over the runway, the pilot can reduce speed and drop down to about a foot or so above the landing surface. With the throttle closed, he can gently pull back on the joystick, putting the aircraft in the three-point-landing position while making sure that the relative position of his aircraft in the broad scene does not change and is not allowed to climb. With the stick pulled right back, the airspeed would have dropped to aircraft stalling speed and the landing wheels would gently touch the runway and a perfect landing would result.

If the pilot had tried to put the wheels on the runway before stall speed was reached, the aircraft would bounce and he would have to recover flying speed with a burst of engine power, and in effect, would have to land again farther down the runway, or he would have to go-around-again if there was insufficient room and make another landing attempt.

Because of all the bad weather that we had experienced over the past few weeks, we were behind schedule in our flying training, and all forty-eight-hour passes were reduced to thirty-six hours for the balance of the course. We had been working eighteen-hour days in spite of the weather, which prevented us from doing some of the flying such as aerobatics and cross-country navigational exercises. I had not taken any leave at all since the course started, but I had planned to take a forty-eight-hour leave over the coming weekend.

I had planned to visit Toronto with Alec Ince, travelling by taxi. We would leave Friday night after duty, drive all night, giving me Saturday and Sunday until noon to visit my girlfriend and my father. We would then drive non-stop back to St. Hubert, arriving late in the evening so that we would get adequate sleep and be ready for flying Monday morning. It was a long trip from St. Hubert to Montreal and then on to Toronto along old Highway No. 2. This was long before Highway 401 was built and travelling became much easier. We definitely needed a forty-eight-hour leave for such a long trip.

We decided to carry on with our plan and ignore the order restricting all leaves to thirty-six hours. We pooled our money to hire the taxi so that it did not cost too much. The taxi picked us up at the gate at about eight o'clock and we headed for Montreal.

After driving for about three hours, the driver claimed that he was tired so I took over the wheel. Alec and I shared the driving throughout the night. The driver had the best of the deal, taking over the driving after sleeping all night as we came into the Toronto outskirts.

We saw our friends and relatives and got back together again just before noon on Sunday. The taxi driver picked us up and we commenced the journey back to St. Hubert. We again took turns driving and arrived at the base late in the evening.

Since we did not have a proper leave pass we could not enter by the regular gate, so we had to climb the fence a few hundred yards from the gate. We were not challenged at all which was normal for Canadian airfield security, and we were able to get to bed in our barracks as planned.

In the morning, we found out that there had been a personnel count and they knew that two students were missing late Sunday afternoon, but they did not know who they were, just that the count was short. They threatened to punish the complete course, so we reported to the chief of flying and confessed that we were the guilty ones. I don't remember what our punishment was, probably twenty-one days C.B. (confined to barracks), but it was in name only as we continued on our eighteen-hour duty days right through to Wings Parade. After flying all morning, attending ground school in the afternoon, followed by the Link Trainer until after eleven at night, being confined to barracks for the remaining six hours while we slept was certainly not a hardship and apparently, once again, my standing in the class was not affected.

As I think back now, I remember my son George having a favourite saying, "I'll be the decider!," obviously taking directly after my own character. At the time I did not really realize it, but all through the war, when decisions had to be made quickly and my life was at stake, I always insisted that, "I would be the decider," and I would do it my way. Perhaps that is why I survived.

Eventually the course was completed, and we could all relax. Wings Parade was December 19, 1941. An Air Vice-Marshall from air force headquarters in Ottawa, pinned wings on my tunic and I was finally a pilot. I was given a three-week leave before going overseas. But before returning to Toronto, my fiancée Diana and I, with Alec Ince and his girlfriend, celebrated the completion of the year-long training by having dinner at the Roof Gardens Dining Lounge on top of the Mount Royal Hotel in Montreal.

Diana Liddle and I were married on December 23, 1941, in Erskine United Church in west-end Toronto. Mr. and Mrs. Humphreys held the reception at their home on Maclean Avenue in Toronto's Beach area. We spent Christmas and New Year's in our own rented apartment in Toronto.

The author and fiancée Diana Elizabeth Liddle. Wings Parade, December 19, 1941. No. 13 S.F.T.S., St. Hubert, Quebec.

I wanted to fly on operations and had no interest in instructing. I believed, "Those who can—do. Those who can't—teach." Of course someone had to instruct to supply the pilots needed to win the war—but not me. Much later on, when I had done my share of operational duty and I was perhaps even injured, I might be willing to pass on what I had learned, but this was not the time. A pilot named Beardall who had been in my course at St. Hubert, was posted to instructor's school at Trenton, Ontario. A few weeks later, when I was at Bournemouth in southern England, I heard that he had been sitting in a Harvard, waiting at the end of the runway in preparation for take-off, when another Harvard landed right on top of him and he was killed.

3. Going Overseas

In what seemed no time at all my leave had come to an end and I left Toronto by train for Halifax, Nova Scotia to proceed overseas. Due to a wild snow storm, the train was many hours late. I found myself in the R.C.A.F. Manning building in Halifax at about three o'clock in the morning trying to complete the necessary paperwork regarding my recent marriage and the swearing-in ceremony for my officer's commission.

By seven o'clock in the morning, I was aboard the troop transport ship, *Stratheden* and I only hoped that my luggage had made it aboard too. By eight o'clock, we were sailing out of Halifax Harbour with one other smaller ship and a destroyer escort. The *Stratheden* was a large and luxurious ship. Before the war it had been in the South Atlantic and Caribbean cruise service.

The troops on board were exclusively air force—2,600 plus sergeant pilots and other aircrew, and 28 or so officers. Except for the actual handling of the ship, which was done by seamen, the ship was just like an air force station, complete with a commanding officer, adjutant and orderly room. Before we boarded the ship, a senior air force officer had given us quite a rousing talk; something like, "If I were twenty years younger, I would be going with you brave men, etc. etc." He then shook hands with every one of us as we moved up the gangplank. I was given a small stateroom on an upper deck, which was quite pleasant. It had a bed that had a movable wooden side gate to keep you from falling out onto the floor in rough weather as I was to learn later.

I was up on the top deck when a Stranraer Flying Boat flew over, reminding me of the flight I took here almost a year ago. It was no doubt searching for enemy submarines to make sure that the convoy was not interfered with. Looking back over the stern of the ship, I could see from the white frothy wake, that the ship was following a zigzag course, turning left and then right at probably five-minute intervals to make torpedo attack difficult for any enemy submarines which may be lurking in its path. The sea was fairly calm and that night we enjoyed the five-course dinner in the luxurious dining room. The next day the wind picked up and the waves were about thirty feet high. We walked up and down on the top deck alongside the giant funnel for exercise. The ship was rolling violently from side to side and pitching from end to end. The stern of the ship would sink down deep in the water, then rise right out of the water with the propellers spinning in mid-air and the engines roaring, while the bow buried itself into a big wave. After a few seconds, the ship would pitch back, the propellers would bite into the water again and the engines would slow under the load. It wasn't too bad for a while but it certainly got on my nerves eventually.

That night, I fastened the side gate in place on my bed and spent the next hour being bounced from one side to the other. At about two o'clock in the morning, someone knocked on my door and advised that since I was orderly officer for the day, would I please come down to the galley where they were having problems. It was news to me that I was orderly officer. I suppose I should have checked at the orderly room yesterday. Since up until a little over three weeks ago, I had been a student pilot, with the second lowest rank in the air force, I had no idea what the orderly officer's duties were on a regular base, never mind on a ship. At St. Hubert I saw the orderly officer only at mealtimes, when after the duty sergeant had brought the room to attention, the orderly officer would step forward and ask,"Are there any complaints." I was pretty sure that they did not want me for that purpose at two o'clock in the morning.

I dressed quickly and stepped outside. No wonder I had been thrown around the bed so violently; there was a real storm raging over the North Atlantic and the waves were now about sixty feet high. The duty sergeant was waiting for me and we hurried down to the galley. The sight of the galley was unbelievable. Great quantities of water were washing back and forth on the deck carrying dozens of pots and pans, roasts of beef and other food stuffs. Everyone looked at me, waiting for me to say something brilliant but really I didn't have a clue. I turned to the sergeant and suggested the obvious, "You will have to get some men to pump out the water and clean up the mess." I am sure that he already knew that but required the authority of the orderly officer to commit the men. He was away like a shot to arrange the clean-up crew.

When he came back with the men, he and I inspected the rest of the ship. Every deck seemed to have a foot or more of water swishing back and forth as the ship rolled and pitched in the storm. Luckily, the aircrew sergeants were fast asleep in their hammocks, slung high above the swirling waters. I could see no need to wake them. It seemed to me that their sleeping hammocks appeared far superior to the "child's crib" that I had been trying to sleep in.

In the morning I went up on the top deck and could not see the second troop ship or the escorting destroyers. They had apparently dropped behind in the storm and we were steaming ahead on our own. I was never really seasick during the voyage, but I never really felt all that good either. Very few people came into the dining room now and it was a battle to get through dinner. The ship was still being tossed about violently in the storm. Coffee cups and soup bowls had to be half-filled or the liquid would splash over onto the table.

The table had a raised edge all around to prevent plates and bowls sliding off, but everyone had to hold on to their soup bowls or they would slide right across the table the next time the ship rolled, hit the opposite raised edge and dump the soup into someone's lap. It happened twice before we caught on.

On the eighth day we were approaching Ireland. I was on the top deck when a flight of Spitfires flew over. I could hear their Rolls Royce engines throbbing away. They certainly were impressive. We sailed around Ireland and late that night we docked at Greenock, Scotland.

In the morning we disembarked to proceed by train to Bournemouth on the south coast of England. The trip took nineteen hours with most of the time spent sitting in sidings while the higher priority freight trains roared by on the main line. We were new arrivals, not yet allotted a function in the overall war machine. We did have a problem with food. The sergeants were given rations, but the officers were apparently on their own and expected to buy their food. The problem was that every station stop seemed to have only watercress sandwiches. It was fine for a while, but they really weren't very nourishing and nineteen hours was a long time without protein. They had nothing else though and we did not have time to walk into town to see if we could find something better. As a result, we subsisted on cups of tea and the weird watercress sandwiches until we got to Bournemouth.

We were billeted in one of the many hotels in this resort town, right on the English Channel. Very early the next morning, a flight of Focke-Wulf 190 Fighter-Bombers attacked the hotel, dropping several bombs which destroyed one complete wing with many fatalities. The coastal guns opened up, but too late to prevent the enemy getting away at wave-top height.

We certainly were not too impressed with our welcome so far. I was very impressed, though, with the enemy's low level tactics. After the bombs exploded, I leaped out of bed and rushed to the window in time to see the enemy aircraft, serenely, I thought, flying back over the Channel with the flak exploding hundreds of feet above them. This display stayed with me and strongly influenced my own low level operational career later on.

Bournemouth was a Manning pool where aircrews were stationed until they were posted to operational training units and on to operational squadrons in England or overseas to the Middle East. My goal was to stay in England where I considered the real battle to be and fly the very best and most modern aeroplanes. They told us that unfortunately for those that did not want to go East, postings would be slow, mainly because of aircraft shortages, unless they wanted to help the air force pioneer the development of new troop-carrying gliders for General Browning's Airborne Division.

In the First World War, wealthy Canadian citizens were encouraged to fund complete military units to help win the war. The Eaton family, and in particular John Eaton, operating Eaton's department stores, formed and funded the operation of the Eaton Motor Machine Gun Battery. My father joined this battery and served in the front line trenches in France as a machine gunner. His advice to my brother and I was, "Never Volunteer!" Both my brother and I had already broken his rule by joining the air force and here I was about to break it again. They promised that it would be a short-term duty, far more fun than sitting in Bournemouth, and the benefit to the war effort would be immeasurable. In any case, I found myself volunteering to help with the development of this motorless aircraft for better or for worse.

My father on dispatch rider duty astride a vintage First World War motorcycle.

Eaton Motor Machine Gun Battery under canvas. Caesar Hill, Folkstone, England. My father, June 1915.

4. Flying Motorless Aircraft

For the next few weeks, I flew General Aircraft Hotspur Training Gliders towed by Hawker Hector, or Hart biplanes at the end of a 200-foot nylon rope, mostly from grassy airfields. The gliders did not have the sailplanes' ability to gain or maintain height by using rising air currents, but were quite heavy aircraft. Although made of wood, they steadily lost height as soon as disconnection to the tow plane was made. The Hotspur Glider, when released from the tow plane at 20,000 feet, was able to glide for up to eighty miles. We used to put the gliders through their paces, trying just about every manoeuvre, including mild aerobatics. But the usual and intended manoeuvre was simply to be towed close to the selected landing point, released and touched down quickly and safely, so that the troops would be in good condition to disembark and confront the enemy. We flew the Hotspur Gliders at Netheravon and Kidlington and the Horsa Operational Gliders at Brize Norton, all located generally in central southern England.

One day when I was at Kidlington, my brother Norm landed on the grass field in his Lockhead Hudson Medium Bomber. He and his crew had been on a navigational trip over the Irish Sea and after running into bad weather had put down on the airfield. It was pure coincidence that it happened to be the airfield where I was based. In any case, he and his crew stayed the night and we were able to spend the evening together at the local village pub. In the morning, the weather cleared and Norm was able to return to his base. A few days later Norm and I spent a three-day leave in London, visiting Madam Tussaud's Wax Museum, the Nelson monument in Trafalgar Square, Buckingham Palace, and other interesting sites.

A month later, Norm and his crew took off from an airfield on the south coast of England and flew to India via, among other refueling stops, Gibraltar, the Island of Malta, and Cairo, Egypt to fly against the Japanese.

We moved on to Brize Norton which had regular hard-top runways, to fly Horsa Troop Gliders, each of which could carry thirty fully-equipped infantry men with the squad commander and the pilot sitting up front in the cockpit. The gliders were towed by Halifax and Sterling Heavy Bombers and sometimes Dakota Aircraft on actual operations.

For a period, while flying Horsa Gliders at Brize Norton, I was appointed squadron welfare officer. This was in addition to my flying duties and was done mostly in my off hours. I did not like it at all, but the air force did not really care if you liked a duty or not. They required an officer to head up each section, whether he knew anything about it or not.

The job involved advising wives when their pilot husbands were injured or killed, making out passes for N.C.O.s to visit their sick family members and generally helping to handle all the private problems of the men and women in the squadron. As I said, not an enjoyable job. I even was given a marital problem that one of my fellow pilots was having with his wife. The wife lived in northern England and had a job in an aircraft factory. Apparently they had only been married a year and now she preferred a man who worked with her in the factory, rather than her husband. I don't remember how it got to court, but it did, and the Judge ruled that there would be a six-month separation with the girl staying away from both her husband and her fellow worker. She wasn't told to quit her job, so the separation applied only to her husband. Within the month her husband crashed and was killed, and I suppose in a very distorted manner, justice was served.

I felt that I was completely ill-equipped for this job. My life had been quite ordinary and uncomplicated. I knew nothing of the way life really was. I was relieved when eventually another poor unsuspecting pilot was appointed to the job.

The first glider operation attempted was an attack on a radar station in Norway, utilizing two Horsas, towed by Halifaxes. Two

Australian pilots from our R.A.F. group, flew the gliders. They trained for the operation in Scotland which simulated the Norwegian terrain. For some strange reason that none of us understood, although all the training had been done below 4000 feet, the actual operation called for flying over the North Sea at 10,000 feet. Before they reached the coast of Norway, one of the towing ropes broke, no doubt because it had frozen solid due to the altitude. The glider pilot managed to stretch his glide, so that he did reach land, but as he attempted to touch down on the Norwegian beach, the glider and all on board were destroyed by the enemy coastal guns.

The second Horsa didn't fare any better. As the glider, towed by the Halifax, approached the radar site, they both experienced very heavy anti-aircraft fire including small arms fire, which cut right through the wooden walls of the glider and caused both to crash to the ground with no survivors. Only one Halifax bomber returned to base from this operation.

Gliders were used on several Allied assaults, including Sicily, Normandy and Arnhem, with some success but always pointing out the serious weaknesses of which we were already aware. Firstly, gliders should not have been used in an operation unless, and until, we had air and ground superiority. Secondly, army glider pilots should have been far better trained. Air force pilots, with their breadth of flytraining, could handle the many variations of conditions which confront a pilot each time he lands or takes off, so that he can adjust to suit. The army pilots, with their very limited training, were far too slow and "wooden" in reacting to situations.

During the Sicily Invasion, the landing of troops by glider on the island was unopposed, except for a few timid Italian squads, and should have been a textbook deployment. Instead, because there was a strong wind blowing offshore, none of the gliders made it to land—all put down in the water. How the hundreds of troops with their equipment made it to shore I cannot imagine, but it could not have been easy. The Horsa Gliders had very good landing flaps. The pilots should have been able to adjust their glide path to ensure they were over land before deploying full flap at the last minute to touch down exactly on target regardless of the wind. The rule was to always be sure that you were going to overshoot your selected landing spot before releasing the tow cable and then use flaps to get rid of excess height. Full flaps would bring you almost straight down— there should have been very little guesswork required. Height is the most valuable asset when flying motorless aircraft and should never be squandered. Once lost, you could never regain the height. Your only mode of power was gravity and you had to use it to maintain flying speed once separated from the tow plane.

The Airspeed Horsa operational glider.
Source: *An Illustrated History of the R.A.F.* ©1990 Colour Library Books Ltd., Keystone Collection

During the development of glider tactics, we found that putting many gliders down into small fields was not a problem, yet, when I flew over a field to observe an army glider landing exercise, there was a solitary tree in the centre of the field and three gliders had managed to hit it. Obviously more training or faster reactions, or both, were required.

We did not do any of the mass flying instruction. We provided some training for just a few army officers and senior N.C.O.s and the army planned to have them train the balance of the division.

At this time, the old bugbear of increased flying accidents began to creep into the program. One day when we were having tea, a Hotspur Glider crashed on the lawn in front of the officers' mess. There were five soldiers on board rather than just the pilot and co-pilot. The glider literally disintegrated leaving injured soldiers lying on the grass with wooden pieces from the glider protruding from some. All lay quietly. No one made a sound. The squadron doctor, who had been in the mess, ran from man to man examining and shouting orders to ensure that those that could be saved received care, while those that were too badly injured were, at least temporarily, ignored. Why the glider pilot dived into the middle of the lawn, I just don't remember.

Another accident involved a Hotspur getting caught in the trees bordering the airfield, dragging down the tow plane. For some reason neither could release the tow rope.

About this time the King and Queen of England visited the airfield and a glider deployment and a paratroop drop display were presented. A Whitley bomber, loaded with paratroopers was on its take-off run on the grass field when it lost power on its left engine. This caused it to veer ninety degrees to the left towards the line of hangars. The Whitley was under-powered even with two engines operating, so the pilot should have immediately aborted the take-off, shut down the right engine and if necessary, if still going too fast, pulled up the undercarriage. Instead, the pilot, unbelievably, decided to continue the take-off run and attempt to climb over the hangars. With only one engine operating and the very heavy load of the paratroopers, he didn't have a chance and crashed deep into the wall of the hangar. Fire broke out immediately, and except for three of the paratroopers who appeared at the rear door of the aircraft after we managed to pry it open, all others on board perished. Of the paratroopers that jumped that day, two Roman-candled; that is, their parachutes tangled, failed to open and they were killed.

The General Aircraft Hotspur Training Glider.
Source: *An Illustrated History of the R.A.F.* ©1990 Colour Library Books Ltd., Keystone Collection

At this time, I felt that whether or not I had helped in this program, it was time that I moved on. I had heard that North American Aircraft in the United States had developed a new fast aeroplane for the Royal Air Force, called the P-51 Mustang, to be used in their low-flying photographic reconnaissance squadrons of Tactical Command. Although my photographic knowledge began and ended with my little Brownie Snapshot camera, I decided that this was exactly what I had been waiting for. When I remembered how the enemy planes had sneaked in to bomb the hotel in Bournemouth and then made fools of the gunners as they flew back over the Channel completely unscathed, I realized that this strategy should work very well for the new Mustang squadrons.

P-51 Mustang.
Source: *Action Stations, Volume 5. Military Airfields of the South-West.* © R.C.B. Ashworth 1982.

5. Operational Training Unit: Mustangs

Because the army had, for better or for worse, taken over the glider pilot training, it was not too difficult for me to remove myself from the program, which I did with great haste and a sense of relief.

I visited Air Ministry in London and spoke to them regarding what was happening. They obviously knew all about it and gave me exactly what I wanted. I could hardly believe that they gave me an immediate posting to Howarden Operational Training Unit, near Chester in northern England for training on Mustangs.

I found that flying the Mustang was a fantastic difference to flying the motorless gliders. After disconnecting the tow rope, the glider floated silently around the sky, always, of course, coming down until softly touching down on the grass exactly as planned. The first time I flew the Mustang, I opened the throttle to take off down the runway and was astounded at how hard my back was pressed against the seat as the speed rapidly increased. By the time I had reached down to raise the wheels and a small amount of take-off flap, the airfield was about a mile behind me. As I flew around the landing circuit to land on the runway again, I had so much to do in the cockpit, checking all instruments, adjusting the propeller pitch and fuel mixture with the engine's powerful roar in my ears, that I did not have time to look around at all. In what seemed a matter of seconds, I was approaching the airfield again and had to lower the undercarriage and full flap to touch down on the runway, still travelling at a speed far in excess of the top speed of any of the gliders recently flown.

The Mustang was everything that I thought it would be—very fast and manoeuverable, although, I was very disappointed in the operational tactics taught. They were vintage 1940 Battle of Britain, complete with "Vic" and "Line Astern" formation flying—no doubt adequate for Spitfire Fighter Squadron operations, but hardly what I was looking for. Low flying practice was very timid and not really low at all. I had flown much lower back in St. Hubert. I was not operational myself yet, but I had been on bases in southern England during *Luftwaffe* attacks, including Bournemouth, where I was able to observe their low level tactics and knew that what they were teaching at this school would be useless in this new air war. I, therefore, spent most of my time learning to fly the aeroplane as expertly as I could and resigned myself to learning tactics later, the hard way, while flying actual missions. Luckily, although the Operational Training Units were lagging, the Operational Squadrons, at least the one I joined, employed the very latest tactics devised from daily engagement with the *Luftwaffe*.

While training at Howarden, we were able to visit the town of Chester several times in our off hours. Chester had a wall all the way around it, built by the Romans, upon which you could walk while sightseeing. We would walk along, eating very-well-prepared fish and chips, which were delicious. For some weird reason, they were always wrapped in a cone of ordinary newspaper. The ink didn't seem to affect the taste, though.

Following completion of training, I managed to retain my above-average flying rating, in spite of spending the past few months flying aircraft without engines. I and my two friends were posted to 268 Squadron based at New Market in southeastern England.

6. The Squadron

268 Squadron was a Royal Air Force Photographic Reconnaissance Squadron of Tactical Command, flying P-51 Mustangs and later Typhoons. The aircraft were designed to carry large motor-operated cameras mounted behind the pilot in a horizontal position, left or right, in the coupe top for the taking of line-overlap oblique pictures at zero feet. A camera could also be mounted vertically with the lens pointing straight down through the bottom of the fuselage, to take vertical pictures, usually at 37,000 feet, again on a line-overlap basis. A one-hour flight could produce a fantastic overview of just about the whole of Europe, so this type of mission was seldom required.

The aircraft were very fast for the time, faster than the ME109 and equal or better than the latest version of the Focke-Wulf 190. We were equipped with the latest version of the Mustang, and later, the Typhoon as they came off the production lines.

Armament was four 20mm. Hispano Cannons used for defence when on reconnaissance and for offence when on other missions. The loading mix of shells would be armour-piercing, explosive and incendiary repeated, giving tremendous fire-power to each individual Mustang.

The main function of our squadron was reconnaissance and once pictures were taken, the objective was to get them back to base as quickly as possible—direct action by other groups depended on them. Taking time to engage in other actions, however tempting, was frowned upon, to say the least, as you might be shot down and the photographs lost.

When I joined, the squadron's mission was to photograph the entire coastline of Europe from about a mile out from shore and at zero feet, including Norway, Holland, Belgium and France. This also included the coastal ports of Oostende in Belgium, Calais, Le

Havre and Dieppe in France and the Normandy beaches. We did not know at that time, in 1942, that the invasion would be made through Normandy. Even if it had already been decided, we would have had to photograph the whole coast so as not to pinpoint interest in any one area. The invasion was a very well-kept secret and I don't think many people knew anything about it before the final briefing on June 4, 1944. At zero feet, the camera was at about the eye level of the sailors who would be steering the landing craft to the invasion beaches. By referring to our pictures, they would be able to land the troops on the beach where they were required to be. An effective invasion depended upon each craft landing exactly where planned.

The Germans were always very concerned about our activities. Anytime we appeared off the coast, taking pictures, we would be visited by one or more enemy flights bent on stopping us. While we were photographing Le Havre, they opened up with their naval-style guns and volleyed sixteen-inch shells along the surface of the water at us. Following the Canadians' disastrous attack at Dieppe in August 1942, when out of a force of some 5,000 men only a handful were able to get back to England, it was decided not to attempt to take a port in spite of the obvious advantages over an isolated beach. The port could be too easily heavily defended.

Our method of getting the coastline pictures was to arrive over the pre-selected area at 10,000 feet in squadron strength—two flights of nine aircraft. One flight, without cameras, would patrol back and forth to provide cover. The second flight, with cameras mounted, would drop down to 4,000 feet and patrol at that height about a mile out from the coastline to be photographed. These nine aircraft would then, one at a time, dive down to zero feet and photograph the section of the coast allotted to them, more or less like a well-organized football team. One aircraft would be flying dead straight and level on its photographic run, one just completed and one ready to start, so that coverage would be certain to overlap and continuous line-overlap sets of photographs would be obtained.

If and when the enemy tried to interfere with the picture-taking, an aircraft from the top flight would attack with guns blazing to drive the enemy aircraft away and rather than press the attack, would break off and quickly return to the top cover flight in case of another attack. In this way, we were able to allow the aircraft, taking their three-minute photographic runs, time to concentrate on picture-taking only. Usually the Germans did not press the attack either, and seemed satisfied to attack the bottom flight, who would take evasive action, while the top flight, if necessary, when more than one enemy aircraft was involved, would dive down from 10,000 feet with their superior speed and fire-power and easily drive them away leaving the photographic aircraft undisturbed.

Sometimes we were not so lucky, and we would have a pilot down in the channel. In this case, we would call "Mayday" on our emergency channel for Air-Sea rescue. Air-Sea rescue was a small Walrus flying boat which was completely defenseless. We had to provide protective cover for the time it took to accomplish the rescue. When the sea was too rough for the flying boat to land and get off again safely, it was up to the pilot to get into his dinghy and hope that a Motor Torpedo Boat Squadron would pick him up. All we had time and fuel to do was to give them his position. If the pilot drifted too close to the enemy coast he was on his own.

Many times we had to abort the mission if the attack was too strong, or if any of the aircraft taking the pictures were lost. It took three attempts to photograph Oostende Harbour in Belgium. On one attempt our group captain was shot down into the North Sea. He should not have been flying with us at all. It was April, 1944 and he had recently been briefed on the coming Second Front Invasion—obviously this information would be invaluable to the enemy. If he had been captured, the Gestapo would, no doubt, have done everything they could to get that information. There was a heavy fog and when it lifted, there was a heavy sea in the North Sea for the next five days. Although we searched for him every day in squadron strength, the waves were high enough to hide his dinghy from us each time we flew over him. The dinghy was bright yellow, too. The fifth day, the sea calmed and he was picked up by a Royal Navy Torpedo Boat Squadron. He was not too happy with us when he finally got back to the squadron. He insisted on speaking to us before going to the hospital. He told us that he watched us do beautiful search patterns right over his dinghy every day without once seeing him. I can remember the propeller causing spray from the waves on that search—we couldn't have been lower. He told us that he strangled a seagull and then couldn't eat it. He didn't actually tell us how we should have done the search, though. Perhaps our speed was a disadvantage in this case and we should have used Tiger Moths.

I am being facetious and referring only to the advantage of the very low-flying speed of the Tiger Moth. But, since we had to search close to the Belgium coast, anything but a Mustang or an equivalent fighter would have been quickly destroyed by the hordes of enemy fighters based on the nearby coastal airfields. By the middle of 1942, none of the non-front line aircraft, such as the Hurricane or early versions of the Spitfire, dared to venture out of the United Kingdom. They were shipped out for use in the Middle East or Indian war theatres where they still were a match for the enemy's aircraft.

Photographing Oostende Harbour was such a problem for us that the scientists came up with a high-speed camera that could take many more individual picture frames than before over the same time period, enabling the aircraft to fly much faster across the harbour mouth and still obtain very clear pictures and adequate overlap. The defending gunners would not expect us to be flying at this increased speed, the scientists reasoned, and perhaps we would not lose so many aircraft.

I was selected for this sortie and, in the briefing, was instructed to take the pictures at exactly 500 m.p.h. and as low as possible, to ensure synchronization with the camera motor speed. Although I was told what had to be done, how the job was done was up to me. The top speed for the Mustang was about 440 m.p.h. Flying at speeds above 400 m.p.h. was reserved for real emergencies and for short durations. Maintaining top speed for five minutes or over required notification to the squadron engineering officer, resulting in an engine tear-down and inspection. Obviously then, I had to generate the additional speed of 100 m.p.h. by diving down from some height. I always preferred to practise my ideas over England before putting them into play against the enemy as I did not want to have to repeat the sortie to get it right. I took off to experiment with the problem and thought that I would try diving down from 5,000 feet with 30° of flap down to hold the speed at the required 500 m.p.h. close to the ground, then as the speed dropped off, bring up the flaps slowly to perhaps 15° or 10° to gradually reduce the drag, so that the speed remained constant for the three or four minutes required for the photographic run. The flaps were at zero degrees when level with the underside of the wings and could be hydraulically lowered to 90° when they would be at right angles to the wing. The first 8° provided lift only and no drag. We utilized the 8° setting mainly in order to get the aircraft off from short runways. The remaining 82° of travel produced drag only and was used to provide braking when landing. I had realized the non-linear character of the flap, but I thought that I would be utilizing only the drag portion and would have no problem. Unfortunately when I brought the flap up to 10°, the speed was still dropping and I had to continue into the non-linear area where upon the drag abruptly changed to lift. Because of the extra high speed this produced extra high lift and I was unable to prevent the aircraft rising 100 feet or so. If this had been the actual operation, I would have ended up with great pictures of the sky but not much else.

I gave up the air brake method. After some more experimenting, I left the flaps in the fully-up position, while closing the throttle about half way and diving down from 3,500 feet to bring the speed up to the required 500 m.p.h. at ground level. I then kept the aircraft straight and level and at constant height while slowly easing the throttle forward to keep the speed constant at 500 m.p.h.. I was able to continue for a little over three minutes before I reached the end of the throttle forward travel and the speed started to drop off. According to the scientists, this would accommodate the necessary film length for the job, including the extra pictures they now wanted of a radio direction finding station located beside the harbour.

They wanted the job done in the middle of the day to obtain the maximum light, so I prepared to take off the next day at 1300 hours, if the weather allowed.

The next day the weather was just about perfect when I took off with my No. 2 and two other Mustangs heading for Oostende. We flew out over the North Sea at 3,500 feet rather than trying to sneak up at zero feet and then having to climb to 3,500 feet over Oostende and fool no one. Leaving the three aircraft to provide top cover, I dived down fairly steeply, as I had practised after half-closing the throttle, to level off just short of the R.D.F. station at the required 500 m.p.h. and began my run across in front of the station. I was as low as I could get. As I flew across the many asphalt roadways leading to the station, the aircraft was buffeted by the uneven upcurrents of air and my head took a real beating against the top of the coupe top. The black asphalt roadways absorbed the heat from the sun, producing strong up currents; whereas the grass between the roadways reflected the sun's heat so that there were no rising air currents. The effect in the cockpit was similar to riding a bicycle over railway ties. At the very high speed and being low to the ground the jolts from the updrafts were short but very violent. I managed to reach down and switch the camera on, as I approached the R.D.F. station and began the photographic run. I couldn't take my eyes off the air speed indicator or the ground scene ahead to observe if the pilot light was on, but I did hear the click of the camera shutter and the high speed whine of the motor as the film was moved forward, so I knew that I was taking pictures. Almost immediately I crossed over the last roadway and headed out over the harbour. The water produced no upcurrents, the buffeting stopped, and I was flying smoothly. I was able to hold everything steady, making sure that I included the whole of the harbour, while pushing the throttle farther and farther forward to keep the speed at exactly 500 m.p.h. The gunfire had followed me for the whole of the run across the harbour mouth, but remained some distance behind my tail. My extra speed had succeeded in fooling the defending gunners and, as the scientists had expected, my aircraft was not hit. I switched off the camera and turned for home as the top cover Mustangs dropped down to join up with me. We had had the upper hand with the Germans this time. It probably wouldn't last unless we continued to use all of our resources to plan to always have a trick or two up our sleeve.

When we arrived back at base, the scientists were waiting for us. The film was processed and in spite of the rough ride I had had, I must have been able to at least dampen the buffeting adequately, as the pictures were excellent. I only hoped that the scientists wouldn't return the following week and suggest that we take the pictures at 600 m.p.h. There is a limit to what you can do with just the help of gravity. They did not return at all which meant that they were either completely satisfied with our coverage of Oostende or were turning their attention to Normandy, most probably the latter.

Oostende had always been a particular hot-spot for our squadron. Besides having many of our pilots shot down there, including our group captain, we also had other problems stemming from attempts to photograph this port. Shortly after I joined the squadron, a British flight sergeant pilot was being held for court martial for L.M.F.—lack of moral fiber or cowardice. I cannot remember his name, as usual, or the details of the charge, but it appeared to involve his being chased back over the North Sea following a photographic sortie to the port. He had been flying No. 2, and his No. 1 had been shot down. When I heard that he had nearly completed a tour of operations on the squadron, I really wondered how he could now be accused of lack of anything. Perhaps he had just been badly out-numbered. Having just joined the squadron and not yet operational myself, I tended to be very sympathetic to the flight sergeant. Even after all he had done to serve his country, if he was found guilty he could be dishonourably discharged and be in a far worse position than someone who had not volunteered to do anything for his country.

Later on when I became more experienced, I was acutely aware of the consequence of a No. 2 deserting his leader when attacked. A two-man Mustang unit was proven to be a pretty formidable adversary even against a larger force of enemy fighters. But a lone Mustang was extremely vulnerable if attacked and was left with just about no way of escaping destruction.

Unfortunately, from time to time, a No. 2 failed to support his leader and the only thing to do was to remove the person from operations immediately and post him to where he would not have that type of responsibility, such as instructing, so that no member of the squadron would be in jeopardy. It would be done long before it got to the court martial stage.

I heard later that the flight sergeant had turned back and aborted many of his sorties. This was a sure sign he was unsuitable, as most pilots will go out of their way to fly an operation, including overlooking magneto drops far in excess of that allowed. As for the fact that he was chased back over the North Sea was concerned—that meant nothing. We were instructed to get back with our pictures and not get involved if we could help it. I had been chased out of France many times after getting my pictures, but I would do everything possible to get out as a team. Since we normally flew in a two-aircraft unit, we were invariably out-numbered, as the enemy fighters operated in flights or squadrons. My standard reaction to being jumped by the enemy was to call my No. 2 to alert him and instruct him to close in and follow, whereupon I would break in the direction of the attack and go onto the offensive by attacking head-on with all guns firing. This never failed to disperse them and in the resulting confusion, my No. 2 and I would dive to the deck and rely on our speed and expertise in very very low flying to outrun them.

Luckily, most Focke-Wulf 190 pilots were rather inept at low flying because, in contrast to us, they almost always flew at high altitudes.

As young inexperienced officers we were requested to attend all court martials, not as participants, but as observers. After all the evidence had been presented on both sides, but before the judge had brought down his verdict, we would be asked for our verdict. Our verdict would have no effect on the official proceedings, but would help make us better acquainted with *King's Regulations For Air* which dictated what would be done under the various Royal Air Force situations with little or no interpretation being necessary or allowed.

The squadron engaged in many other activities; some were tactical, which produced immediate results, and some were strategic, where the benefit came later. These included, Rhubarbs which were daytime low level sweeps employing six or nine aircraft abreast in line battle formation across France and Belgium to stop all movement of transport, including trains, aircraft, staff cars and troop vehicles. The trains were protected by flak cars—one behind the engine, one at the rear and one in the middle.

We would attack at 90° to the track and hit the front of the engine. We would try not to hit the engineer as we assumed that he was French or Belgian. I saw proof of how successful we'd been, when later, in France, I had to walk everywhere because there were no trains operating. We strafed the coastal enemy air bases so thoroughly and continuously, destroying planes both in the air and on the ground, that they were forced to evacuate to inland bases. It seemed to me to be far more effective than the "Big Wing" method of reducing the size and effectiveness of the *Luftwaffe*.

We also flew Night Rangers, where a single aircraft was sent over at night to stop all enemy traffic that tried to move during darkness. This kept the pressure on around-the-clock and I believe it really paid off when we finally invaded. Although we picked nights when the vision was bright for these sorties, it was still very difficult to judge your height from the ground. I would be firing away at a train engine at what I thought was normal distance and height, when suddenly I would see the tops of the trees flash by and I would be in a last minute pull up, instead of a planned one. The boiler of the engine usually blew up and I had to fly through the debris. I found that I could handle the attack better if I throttled back and slowed down somewhat.

The R.A.F. doctors really had the pilot's interest at heart, or rather, I suppose the betterment of the Royal Air Force. They were continually researching everything we were doing in an effort to improve operations. They felt that we were not getting enough vitamin C during the winter months. They told us that a planned program involving the absorption of ultra-violet rays would be therapeutically beneficial to the health of the pilots. Ultra-violet rays were at the violet end of the light spectrum, beyond the limit of visibility, and could be generated by an ionized gas lamp. A large room was set up for the program, with a high-power ultra-violet lamp mounted on the floor at the center. Starting at three feet from the lamp, concentric circles were painted on the floor at one-foot spacings, out to ten feet from the lamp. Beginning at the ten-foot circle, the pilots would stand in front of the lamp and receive radiation for the length of time called for, usually ten to fifteen minutes, wearing extra dark glasses to protect their eyes. The next day they would move one foot closer to the lamp and stand on the nine-foot circle, and thus, by gradually increasing the radiation, the maximum benefit would be obtained. It was very important to adhere to the distance from the lamp for the established units of time, as the doctors advised that prolonged exposure could be dangerous. A few pilots did not follow instructions and ended up in the hospital with a fever. They were taken off flying for a few days and the C.O. was not happy. I do not know if I was any healthier but I did end up with a very nice tan.

I was very aware of the value of keeping fit and my mind clear and alert while flying in this war environment. Drinking and flying did not mix. As a result, a seven-day leave was really only six days, as I made it a practice to always return to base one day before I had to fly. Even then, I found that being away from flying for seven days had an incredible effect on my reaction time and overall flying skills. You could always spot a pilot who had just returned from a leave; even if he had allowed for the one-day recovery time, he was the nut who was careening all over the sky trying to stay in formation. We would have to give him a wider berth than usual until he recovered his coordination and was fit to fly with. This temporary loss of coordination was no doubt experienced by all pilots but it was more noticeable with Mustang pilots because of the instantaneous control response. If the pilot made a wrong control action, he could not retract it, as the aircraft would have already made the move.

About the summer of 1943, the air ministry doctors advised us that over the past winter months of December, January and February there had been an unusually high number of casualties among pilots who had had to bail out over the English Channel. Apparently ice flows had drifted much farther south than usual, drastically lowering the water temperature. It was thought that the slowness in getting out of the water and into a dinghy was the cause of the high casualties. If the pilot took too long to get his dinghy inflated, he would be too weak to climb in and would soon succumb to the icy water.

Air ministry advised that their medical team had concluded that the pilot had a maximum of thirty seconds to get out of the water, after which he probably could not get out. The group captain was very concerned and ordered all pilots to make sure that they could meet this time limit. Our C.O. organized a trip to a beautiful spot on the Thames River, some twenty miles west of London, where we would have the use of a swimming pool.

We jumped from the twelve-foot-high diving board into the pool to simulate the parachute landing speed. We wore all normal flying gear—battle dress, parachute and Mae West life jacket to make the test realistic. A fighter-pilot style parachute fitted into the bucket seat of the aircraft with the parachute itself serving as the back rest, while the dinghy made the seat cushion the pilot sat on. The procedure was for each pilot to jump off the diving board into the pool, using the parachute's quick release to ensure that it would not fall on top of him and get in the way of retrieving and inflating the dinghy. In actual bail-out, the parachute, when released, would be carried away a few yards by the wind. The Mae West would then be inflated with the CO_2 bottle and the dinghy inflation would commence.

The valve on the Mae West was usually no problem and inflation was just about instantaneous, but the dinghy valve was tricky. If you hurried and opened it wide, the CO_2 would expand too quickly and would probably freeze. You had to inflate the dinghy gradually to prevent this, as once it froze, it took considerable time for the valve to free itself so that inflation could be continued to the point where the dinghy would be firm enough to support your weight.

We took turns jumping off the diving board and although we tried as hard as we could, no one was able to get into his dinghy within the required time of thirty seconds. Even though we tried all afternoon, the best we could do was a little under one minute. Towards the end of the exercise, we were taking longer and longer to get into the dinghy because it took an incredible amount of energy to hoist oneself into the dinghy wearing the water-soaked battle dress and we ended up absolutely exhausted. Tubby Bourne, who as his name implies, was not a lightweight, jumped and took the full thirty seconds just getting back to the surface again. Eventually, he had the dinghy inflated and climbed aboard, only to over balance and fall back into the water. It was not at all easy. We were very sympathetic though, and advised him to plan on a watery grave.

We spent the evening boating on the Thames and tried to forget about this latest problem. We had done our testing in warm, calm pool water. Trying to get into the dinghy under actual conditions of near-freezing water and five-foot waves, within the thirty-second time limit would obviously not be possible.

Although we were not successful in solving this problem, I felt better that I had been made aware of it. I decided that if my engine was damaged during a winter sortie over the continent and was likely to stop running, crossing back over the channel would definitely not be one of the options that I would consider.

A few of the pilots relaxing after the very strenuous dinghy testing.

There was one sortie flown in July 1943, which, had it been flown in a winter month, would have had a much different ending. The sortie was flown by Guy Pease and his No. 2 to obtain low level oblique photographs of one of the many V1 launching sites along the Belgian coast. As Guy and his No. 2 roared across the V1 site, flying straight and level on their photographic run, a large calibre anti-aircraft gun, probably an 88, began firing at them at almost point blank range with the barrel depressed to below level so that it could be aimed at the low flying Mustangs. The shells were exploding between the two Mustangs and they could hear the shrapnel impacting all along the sides of both aircraft. Guy felt a piercing pain in his side and leg and his engine was losing power as he turned towards the Belgian coast. Luckily the sortie involved only a shallow penetration of the continent, so that he and his No. 2 were soon on their way back over the channel. Guy could feel the blood soaking into his battle dress jacket and down his trousers but he had to ignore it, as he had other things to worry about. His engine was losing more and more power and he was getting closer and closer to the water. He called his No. 2, advised that he had to bail out immediately and requested that he "Mayday" for him. Guy then quickly went over the side.

His No. 2 told us later that he was really shocked when Guy advised him that he was bailing out, as his own engine had also been hit at the V1 site and he had expected to have to bail out himself at any minute. He quickly switched his VHF set to the emergency channel, called "Mayday," gave them Guy's approximate position in the channel, but advised that because of his engine problems he would have to return to base immediately and could not wait to assist Air-Sea Rescue, which was normal procedure. He then turned for home and hoped that he could make it.

In the meantime, Guy was in the water and had discovered that he could not inflate his Mae West and when he tried to inflate his dinghy, he was again unsuccessful. Obviously both had been punctured by the shell fragments when he himself was hit. He had no choice but to tread water, but he wondered how long he could keep it up and stay afloat.

The rescue Walrus was dispatched to search for Guy with a Spitfire escort for protection. It was getting dark by the time they arrived in the area. They did a quick search and although the water was as calm as a mill-pond, they were looking for a pilot in a dinghy, unaware that Guy was furiously treading water, waving and shouting as they flew over.

The Walrus pilot knew that he had little or no chance of finding anyone now that it was dark so he flew back to the base and decided to return at dawn.

As Guy told us later, the sound of the aircraft engines fading away was just about the last straw. He knew that they would be back in the morning, but wondered if he could keep his head above water until they arrived. He had the comparatively warm and calm water of the channel in his favour, but he could not help worrying about his side and leg wounds. With the pain and extensive bleeding, aggravated by the vigorous movement of his arms and legs to stay afloat, he was sure that the shell pieces in the wounds were huge and had done extensive internal damage. In any case, he had to forget about his injuries and concentrate on keeping alive for the next four or five hours.

At dawn the rescue Walrus with its escort arrived and began an extensive search. They were still looking for a pilot sitting in his dinghy, not a small bobbing head in the water. They finally spotted the deflated dinghy floating on the surface of the water, which was luckily still nice and calm. The Walrus pilot landed on the water close to where Guy was still treading water, and by now was close to exhaustion. They pulled him aboard, took off quickly and headed for the hospital.

When I visited Guy in the hospital later, I spoke to the doctors. They said that Guy's side injury had been done by a small piece of shrapnel about one-quarter-of-an-inch square and the piece that struck his leg was even smaller and no serious damage had been done at all—thank goodness.

Guy had had the shell fragments removed and the wounds dressed and was now in the recovery ward. For some reason he seemed very tired and kept falling asleep as I talked to him. I suppose the effects of his operation and the fact that he had treaded water all night in the middle of the channel would no doubt account for his sleepiness. I thought that I had better shut up and let him get some well-deserved rest. I couldn't help but wonder though, as I looked down at this completely exhausted fellow, just how many people would have endured the agony for five or six hours without succumbing to the easy way out—giving up and just slipping quietly beneath the water to end the ordeal.

Guy was a comparatively new member of the squadron at this time and I didn't know him very well. What I did know, did not particularly impress me. Guy was not an aristocrat, but was public school educated.

He spoke with a very English accent, always having, it seemed, to have to rearrange several marbles in his mouth to get the words out. He would use weird expressions such as, "Indubitably Old Chap," and other phrases which to me were not even appropriate.

But as I looked down at him on his hospital bed, I had a new respect for him. I realized that the rather boyish, immature, and even frivolous image he presented to the world, certainly covered up his great determination and strength of character. I felt that I would be honoured to fly with this fellow anytime, even though I would not always know what he was talking about.

There was a real need during the war for pilots to do something every few months, which would help them to erase the collection of daily images of death and destruction from their minds in order to be prepared for the next few months' operations.

One method for doing this was playing a game called, "Cardinal Puff." When it was first explained to me, I thought that it was the most ridiculous past-time that I had ever heard of. It involved going through a fairly complicated ritual of motions with your hands touching various parts of your body. Completed without a mistake would make you "Pope." Each mistake would mean that you would have to begin the ritual again, after taking a deep drink of beer. I can't remember the exact ritual of hand motions in the game, but it included tapping your forehead with your right-hand index finger, then your left-hand index finger, after saying,

"Cardinal Puff Says," each time a motion is to be made. Tapping the nose, the chin, the knee, the leg, and the ankle always after saying, "Cardinal Puff Says," extended the ritual, leaving plenty of chances to make a mistake.

I was sitting around a table in a pub in London with my friends the first time I reluctantly agreed to participate in this game. Bill Irwin agreed to be the first one to try to be "Pope," and away he went. He completed quite a few of the motions before he made a mistake and had to start again, after taking a good drink of beer from the pint in front of him. In no time at all, he had made another mistake and despite his denial, he had to go back and take another drink before starting again. Over the next three or four minutes he was forced to start over again and again and had consumed so much beer that his pint had to be refilled twice.

I never saw anything like it. While the rest of us were sitting around the table, stone-sober, watching Bill, he was getting higher and higher, making more and more mistakes. We were just about rolling on the floor laughing at him. He thought that he was winning but he was making a mistake at every other word and the more beer he had to drink, the more mistakes he made. Needless to say, Bill did not make "Pope" and eventually we had to pull him back from the table to stop him. Actually no one won the game. It was just about impossible. Being well aware of the effect that beer had on the human brain, I quickly gave up when it was my turn and the mistakes began. I knew that it would be all downhill from that point.

Winning the game was not the objective. I had come to London on a short leave, with my mind almost numb from what had happened over the past few months. After watching Bill make an idiot of himself over the past ten minutes, I really had almost forgotten just what I had been concerned about.

Another pastime, which was equally stupid but also served to keep us sane, was "Fighters and Bombers." This was played in, of all places, the officers' mess. We always changed into battle dress because it was so messy. I don't know how the mess survived.

Of the people in the mess, half would be fighters, the other half, bombers. The fighters would stand in two rows in the middle of the room, each holding a pint of beer. The bombers would run between them, while the fighters tried to hit them with the beer. If you were hit in the face with a full pint of beer, I guarantee that whatever was worrying you earlier, would be banished from your brain and, in spite of the extreme stupidity of the act, you would be refreshed ready to fly again. The advantage of this method was that you didn't have to drink the beer, and could even fly the next day without the usual loss of coordination.

Very early in my career, I was flying in the "Tail-End-Charlie" position in a "Vic" formation lead by Alec Breeze. The mission was to observe and photograph activity on several enemy airfields in the Somme estuary area at 1,500 feet. Whether or not me and my apparent obsession with low flying had anything to do with it, all observation missions were stopped eventually in favour of low level photographing or strafing missions. I was determined to do a good job protecting the formation from enemy fighters, so that I was continually flying back and forth in fine pitch and full throttle. As a result I was using far more fuel than the rest of the flight who were able to cruise along straight and level.

The Mustang had three fuel tanks, one in each wing and one in the fuselage behind the pilot, with a three-way valve on the floor beside the pilot. The procedure was to switch the valve back and forth so that fuel would be taken evenly from the three tanks to maintain aircraft balance so as not to completely drain any one tank, as an air bubble could occur which could cause engine failure.

I was so busy flying my position that I completely forgot about switching tanks and was reminded of it only when the red light came on, the fuel alarm sounded and the engine lost power. My right hand grabbed the fuel wobble pump and I pumped furiously, after switching to a full tank. We had completed observing the enemy airfields and were now out over the Channel when the problem surfaced.

I was dropping lower and lower and falling behind the flight when Alec called me to ask if I was having a problem. I called him to advise that I had a temporary fuel problem but that I would rejoin the flight momentarily. However, no matter how quickly I moved the wobble pump, the engine did not seem to be getting any fuel. I began to think that there must be an air bubble in the line or the wobble pump, blocking the flow of fuel. I was almost on the water when the engine finally picked up power with a roar. I climbed at full power to join up with the flight again and radioed Alec to advise that everything was O.K. I never again failed to operate the fuel valve as required. It was strange, but I seemed to always have to learn things the hard way.

One day I was introduced to a new pilot who had recently joined the squadron. His name was Spooner and he seemed to be a real hot shot. He told me that he just couldn't wait to get on operations and appeared to be champing at the bit to get out of the training flight and into one of our operational flights. He rather reminded me of myself when I joined the squadron many months ago, so I advised him to learn all he could now and that he would be on operations soon enough.

A day or so later, as I walked into the mess to have tea, I passed Spooner on his way out. Although he said hello to me in a normal manner, his overall appearance and attitude had changed drastically. Even his hair, which had been so well-groomed, was sticking out everywhere. I found out that he had had to crash-land in the trees at the end of the runway after his engine quit on take-off. This was during the time of our water-in-the-petrol problem. I made a point of looking up Spooner. After finding out that he wasn't hurt personally, I advised him to consider that any landing where the pilot can walk away is a good landing, so he should forget the crash and get on with his learning. I didn't mind that he had lost some of his cockiness, but I was concerned that he might have also lost his nerve. I was reassured when the wild look in his eyes calmed and he even reached up with his hand to smooth his hair. Anyone who can think about his hair after a crash is fast recovering.

Until I arrived overseas and was posted to my first squadron, I did not smoke cigarettes or even have the desire to. I suppose because all the other pilots smoked, I thought that I must be missing something. So I started to have the odd cigarette but only when I was on leave, not everyday as a regular thing. It was just as well that I wasn't addicted as I would have had a serious problem when I was in France. Cigarettes were not available to the *maquis.* Besides, puffing on a cigarette while moving through the towns and countryside in the dark would have been a dead giveaway.

In England, I bought Churchman cigarettes, which were quite expensive compared to the more popular brand, Woodbines, which were dirt cheap—both were packaged in cardboard packs, without the silver paper liner to keep them fresh. As a result, when I dressed in my best uniform to travel to London or some other town, my pack of Churchman cigarettes would be in the pocket, and when I proudly flourished them and offered them to my friends, there would be a lot of coughing and shouting as they lit up. They wanted to know just how long I had had the cigarettes. I had had the pack in my uniform pocket for three or four months. To be honest, I had not noticed that they were any drier than usual and when Frank Jenkins gave me a fresh replacement cigarette, the improvement was lost on me.

I puttered with the cigarette habit for the next few years until it all came to a head at Bogue Electric of Canada in Ottawa. I was chief engineer with the company and was working very hard on a multi-million dollar contract to supply 400 cycle generating equipment with magnetic amplifier voltage control to the Royal

52

Canadian Navy for installation in twenty-eight new destroyer escort naval vessels being built in various shipyards across Canada.

I had attended a meeting in our boardroom with senior officers of the Department of National Defence and the Department of Defence Production and although the meeting was quite successful, I had smoked so many cigarettes over the past few hours, that I really felt completely exhausted.

It was very late when I left the building to go home. I climbed into my Oldsmobile 88 and as I drove down the driveway to turn onto River Road, I suddenly realized that I was still smoking a cigarette. With disgust, I quickly took it out of my mouth and threw it out the window. The window, however, wasn't open and the still-burning cigarette bounced off the glass right into my lap. I quickly wound the window down, but I couldn't find the cigarette butt. In the confusion, I just about had a head-on collision with a car coming from the opposite direction. Finally, I had to pull over to the side of the road and jump out to get rid of the still-hot butt, which by now had burned a large round hole in the front of my winter coat. That was the last cigarette that I ever smoked. I quit cold-turkey on the spot.

Although I was able to have my coat satisfactorily repaired with the help of "Invisible Mending," I finally realized that there was absolutely nothing good about smoking cigarettes. There was nothing relaxing about inhaling nicotine with the accompanying toxic chemicals. Nicotine is an addictive stimulant which does not make your brain work smarter, but becomes more confused and disoriented, while the toxic chemicals destroy your lungs over the years.

<hr>

A pilot's life in R.A.F. Tactical Command during the war, could be summed up in a few words, "Hurry Up" and "Wait." It was always necessary to get down to dispersal early—in the morning, usually, for all missions except Night Rangers—but due to either the enemy or the weather, he would have to wait in a standby mode until conditions warranted his action. He had to be ready to get airborne within three minutes or less following a "Scramble" alarm, so that he had to stay in the pilot's ready area within earshot of the telephone or the loudspeaker.

Rather than just sitting around waiting, we preferred to play poker. We had to teach the British pilots how to play as their education seemed to be sadly lacking in this area.

We were far from being experts ourselves, but we did know the basics as laid down by Hoyle in his book, so we outlined the rules and the values of the various hands. Soon we were able to get a game going more or less. We established a shilling maximum bet per card, with three raises allowed up to the last card, of the five- or seven-card-stud poker game, where a ten shilling bet with three raises was the limit.

We tried to explain to them the psychological character of the game, where the player with the best hand would not necessarily win each time, as he could be bluffed by another player, who by having very good cards face up in front of him, or by playing extremely confidently, or by simply betting high and raising each time he received a card, managed to convince him that he had a hand, far higher than his. If a player had won the previous hand, and he bet and raised wildly during the next hand, obviously he would gain a psychological advantage and would win again, unless one or more of the other players had exceptionally good cards. In playing the game, each player continually judged his chance of winning by the cards in his hand and the cards face up in front of the other players. If one or more of the players was to start raising the bet, then of course, the other players had to reassess their chance of winning and either meet the raise or fold their hand.

The British pilots never really understood the game. The fact that one hand of poker could be won by perhaps a pair of nines, while the next would require three aces or even a flush to win the pot, seemed to be a mystery to them. It showed in their betting.

One Canadian player would bet, say five shillings at showdown, the next Canadian player would see the five shillings and raise ten shillings. When it came to the British player, he would advise that he would see the five shillings raise, and the ten shilling raise, and would raise again by sixpence. This always caused us to stop the game while we explained to him that any player, after putting in five shillings, and then ten shillings, could not be bluffed out by sixpence.

They invariably paid no attention though, and went blindly on with the bet, winning the hand sometimes, but usually losing. Their bet had no bearing on the value of their hand at all, but probably more on wanting to stay in the game and yet not wanting it to cost them too much.

To the Canadians, the game of poker became more of a lottery than a contest of strategy and bluff. Every time I heard a British pilot follow a ten shilling raise with a shilling, or a sixpence, I really didn't know what to think, and in any case, I was usually wrong.

The understanding, of course, was that the game would terminate as soon as a "Scramble" was called. Many times I found myself really wishing for the termination of a game, which had long ago become nonsensical according to Hoyle's or anybody else's rules. As I roared down the runway to take off, and rotated the aircraft to climb vertically on the propeller to intercept altitude, I often was still trying to ponder why anyone would even think of using such weird tactics in the good old game of poker.

During a Rhubarb which I lead, we were right down on the deck pouring cannon shells into a long truck convoy which we'd encountered deep into France. As we rose up to fly over the convoy, I saw, for the first time, that they were ambulance trucks with big white crosses on their roofs, which I had not seen from low level. I immediately called for my flight to cease firing, but I knew that we had already done extensive damage. Back at the base debriefing, I told the senior officer present about the mistake that I had made. He advised me not to worry about it, as they had proof that the Germans were now using their ambulances more to transport munitions than injured soldiers.

Before flying in to Llambedr, Wales to learn how to guide the Royal Navy Cruiser's guns onto their Irish Sea targets in preparation for D-Day, we were sent down to Lark Hill Army Camp on the Salisbury Plain to practise shooting their twenty-five-pound artillery pieces for a day. We were in radio communication with the gunnery officer; by close-up observation of the target, after calling for a shot, we were able to fly in and quickly get the shots right on the bull's eye.

After a successful shoot, we put down on the camp's landing strip and stayed for high tea. We were of course wearing battle dress and not our dress uniforms, so that we stood out as rather scruffy, compared to the really spit-and-polish army people in the officers' mess. Most of the military at Lark Hill were staff officers, with red flash tabs on their uniform collars and in their hats. They marched everywhere, clicked their heels and ate by numbers, almost like West Point in the United States.

Before returning to our base, the artillery captain drove us over to see Stonehenge, which is at the side of the highway to Salisbury. Stonehenge is the name of the remains of a collection of giant rocks arranged in a more or less semi-circular pattern on the ground facing roughly west. The rock formation was apparently built by the Druids for some astronomic purpose. Examining the set-up, we noticed that as the sun set in the west, its light rays shone through a slot in the rock pile and impinged on a central giant rock. This might have meant something to the Druids, but to date it remains a mystery to the world.

The captain also drove us down the highway to Salisbury for a quick visit. Although I had seen a number of Britain's cathedrals, including St. Paul's in London, I was really impressed with the cathedral in Salisbury, so much so that I returned a few days later, when I could spare the time, and took a low level oblique at about sidewalk height. By more luck than skill I obtained a really excellent picture with the cathedral exactly centred. I probably frightened the people in town, flying so low and fast in front of the cathedral. Our squadron was approved for flying low anywhere, so that there was no danger to anyone and I would not be disciplined, even if reported, although I would have to admit that it was not exactly an operational requirement.

Being the officer in charge of the squadron photographic section at the time, I was able to have the picture enlarged to portrait size. Unfortunately, someone walked off with it when I was on the missing list later on, and I did not get a chance to take it home with me.

Flying out from Odiham Airfield to cross the Channel on our way to France, we often passed over R.A.F. Farnborough Experimental Station, where, among many other things, they were experimenting with jet engine aeroplanes. We used to see them buzzing around over the aerodrome. They were very small craft, very fast, flying in short spurts, soon out of fuel and having to land after very short flights. We were definitely not as far ahead as the Germans, we realized, with their V1s, V2s and later, their ME262 Fighters.

Southern Ireland did nothing to help Britain win the Second World War. They allowed the German submarines to sail into their Atlantic ports for refueling, reprovisioning and even the repairing of battle damage, so that they could go back out into the Atlantic to sink more Allied shipping. Southern Ireland cities were not blacked-out as they were in Northern Ireland during the war. The enemy bombers were able to use the glow of the lights in the south to ensure that they were lined up to drop their bombs more accurately on London. Many Northern Ireland people were valuable members of the British forces. Several months before D-Day the ferry service from the mainland to Northern Ireland was stopped. This was a real hardship to the Irish members in the military, but was necessary to prevent enemy spies, known to be in both Northern and Southern Ireland from learning invasion secrets.

Amongst the many things that all pilots had to remember, if they wanted to stay in one piece while flying on operations, was the function of the I.F.F. unit which was installed in every Allied aircraft. The I.F.F.—Identify: Friend or Foe—unit, when switched on, would transmit a continuous signal in code form—which could be changed daily—which would identify the aircraft as "Friend" and they would not be fired upon. An enemy aircraft flying over the United Kingdom would not be transmitting the signal, so it would be considered a "Foe" and would be brought down.

Allied aircraft, flying on operations over the continent, would switch off the I.F.F. unit as they were outgoing from the English coast, so that they were not tracked by the enemy. Upon returning, they would have to remember to switch the unit on again as they approached the English coast, so that the British coastal artillery would recognize them as "Friend" and allow them safely back home.

When war was declared on Germany on September 3, 1939, all shipping into the United Kingdom was reserved for equipment and materials needed for the execution of the war. By the time I arrived in England, there was an acute shortage of all fruit, vegetables, eggs and dairy products. The only eggs available were the dried powder variety produced in the United States. However, from the local farms in the airfield areas, a limited supply of fresh eggs and pork was available to provide a real bacon and egg breakfast to pilots and other aircrew scheduled for early morning operational sorties over the continent.

The normal British breakfast during the war was powdered eggs, bubble and squeak—cabbage and mashed potatoes, sausages—filled, it was claimed, with a good portion of wood sawdust, or kippers—fried herring—very tasty but impossible to eat—at least for Canadians without a medical degree—without getting a mouth-full of bones. This was a valued treat. I especially enjoyed the operational breakfast before a 4:30 a.m. take-off. It was almost worth getting up for. All other personnel, including pilots and crew not on operational missions, were not entitled to this treat—including even the commanding officer.

268 Squadron under canvas. Pilots, administration and ground crew. Gatwick, May 1944.

The Norwegians had trained their pilots at the Toronto Island Airport with their barracks located on the mainland just across the Western Gap entrance to the Toronto Bay.

The Norwegians fought the war somewhat differently to us. We used to fly operations in all weather conditions unless it was completely socked in. The Norwegians preferred blue sky conditions. Since their country was occupied by the enemy, they also had a much more personal reason for fighting than we did, but they, nevertheless, appeared to have different priorities. One day, one of their squadrons was jumped by the enemy and two of their planes were shot down. They were frothing mad and the next day they went over the continent in wing-strength, looking for a fight—they found one over Belgium. They attacked a squadron of Focke-Wulf 190s and in the ensuing battle, knocked down two and damaged two. That evening they celebrated in the mess late into the night. They were nowhere to be seen the next morning when we lifted off the runway to press on with our rather less glamorous version of "how to win the war."

There was no doubt that the Spitfire was the best aeroplane for high level aerial combat when at short range. It had a very low stalling speed and with its large, elliptical wings providing comparatively low wing-loading, it could execute very tight turns without inflicting too high g-forces on the pilot. In the case of the Mustang and the Focke-Wulf 190, wing-loading and stalling speed was much higher so that the g-force was considerably higher for the same rate of turn. In aerial fighting, the only way you could direct your cannon shells onto an enemy aircraft, with any hope of shooting it down, was to get behind it and turn tighter.

The problem was that as you turned tighter and tighter, trying to get the enemy aircraft into your gunsight, very strong centrifugal forces would build up in accordance with Newton's Second Law of Motion, which would act out from the centre of the circle causing every part of your body to become heavier, up to—depending on the steepness of the turn—two, three, or even six times its weight under normal gravity conditions. When you reached out with your hand to push the throttle lever forward, for instance, sometimes it was all you could do to lift it against the force. The worst effect of the g-forces, though, was the blood draining from the head. With his brain starved of blood, the pilot could make the turn too tight and pass out. This was called a "black-out." There were three distinct stages of the "black-out" which affected the pilot's eyesight in particular; the "red-out," where everything in the scene took on a decided red tinge; the "grey-out," where the cones of the retina would cease operating thus eliminating all colour so that everything looked grey; and the final "black-out" stage, where complete vision would shut down along with everything else and the pilot would lose consciousness. When this happened, the pilot's grip on the joystick, which was keeping the aircraft in the tight turn, would relax, the aircraft would straighten out and the pilot would regain consciousness. In the "grey-out" stage, vision went from quite light grey to very dark grey before blacking out altogether. Since I flew mainly at very low level most of the time, I could not risk staying too long in the dark grey stage as I could not afford losing control. During very violent flying against the enemy, I could be in and out of these "black-out" stages more frequently than I would have liked, but usually survival demanded it.

Since we were invariably outnumbered in our encounters with the enemy, it would have been foolish to do anything but attack head on. I, no doubt, damaged many of them but I never knew for sure. We would usually break off the attack and dive to the ground. It was not good enough to gradually pull out of the dive and fly low level. We had to continue the dive very close to the ground and at the very last second, pull out, hoping that, although we expected to be in the very dark grey vision area, we would remain conscious. Usually the enemy pilots would not follow us down close to the ground and we could fly clear.

A ship sailing through the water of an ocean is only slightly affected by prevailing winds. The force of the wind against the superstructure and the above-water side of the ship will have some affect on the ship's direction, but it will be minimal. The wind causes "standing waves" only on the ocean's surface, similar to a vibrating piano string when a key is pushed down. The ocean waves can be sixty feet or higher, making for fantastic vertical movement, but the mass of water does not move horizontally and so does not affect the course steered. Except for the ocean tides and currents, which must be compensated for to prevent the ship drifting off course, the main mass of the water remains stationary in spite of the wind.

An aeroplane flying through the air is a completely different story. The prevailing wind has a major affect on the navigation of the aeroplane as it is flown from point to point over the earth's surface because it is completely within the moving mass of air—which is the wind itself.

If the pilot has to fly along a track against a head wind, with a tail wind, or if there is no wind at all, he simply has flown the compass course directly. Against a head wind, ground speed is air speed minus the wind speed; with a tail wind, it is air speed plus the wind speed; and with no wind, speed equals air speed.

I was flying a Tiger Moth one very windy day and I made the mistake of getting too far downwind of the airfield before realizing how strong the wind was. The Tiger Moth's top air speed was about 80 m.p.h. and the wind speed was gusting to over 85 m.p.h. back to the airfield. I had to dive into the wind gusts so as not to be blown backwards. Luckily, two of the ground crew arrived at the run to hang onto each wing tip as I put down on the runway. When finally they were able to help me over to dispersal, they had to use tie-downs to prevent the aircraft from being blown away.

The more normal situation in flying is to have to contend with the wind blowing in a direction which would cause the aircraft to be moved to the left or right of the desired track. In order to be able to fly along the track, a force equal and opposite to the force and direction of the wind causing the drift, must be applied. The magnetic course which must be steered is the resultant of the air speed to be flown, and the wind speed and direction. We used a Dalton computer to compute the magnetic courses on our flight plans which included all the various legs of the track, drawn on the map of the country to be flown over, together with large scale maps of the target areas. Navigational landmarks or verification points would be selected, probably one per leg, and circled. These points would be unique to the area so they could be quickly recognized by the pilot as he flashed by at high speed. An intersection of two roads with a railway track or a nearby small lake would be some of the acceptable verification points. Just a road intersection, alone, would not be adequate as there could be dozens of these along the track and the correct one could not be discernible by the pilot.

This type of navigation is known as dead reckoning where the pilot has flown exactly according to his flight plan while visually verifying that he is on track as he is flown directly over, or close to, the landmarks shown on his map. Because of our high speed, our momentum usually carried us through wind gusts, unless they were of gale proportions—which did happen during the winter months—so that course corrections were usually minimal.

To be accurate, and hence successful, dead reckoning navigation required the following: frequent calibration of the aircraft compass; careful computation of the flight plan, courses and leg times; test flying of the first leg of the sortie—from base to the English coast—to determine whether or not the meteorological officer had given me the correct wind speed and direction, which, if incorrect, would require course corrections for all remaining legs; and finally, very careful and accurate flying of the aircraft with no slipping in, or skidding out on turns which could cause cumulative errors to such an extent that the sortie would have to be aborted. The alternative would be to rise up to regain your bearings, but the element of surprise would be lost, the enemy alerted, and your chance of survival would be greatly diminished.

The meteorological officer had a thankless job. He did the best he could with the forecasting data available, but it was usually inadequate. Apparently there are many variables involved in weather forecasting and less than half of these are available or even measurable. Even today the forecasters are unable to get a handle on the rate of change of weather front formation because it is so complex.

When a flying boat, seaplane, or amphibian such as the Walrus, takes off from calm water, the surface tension between the surface of the water and the hull or pontoons causes a very high suction force to work against the lift-off force which is difficult to overcome with the engine power available. The procedure is to first taxi in a large circle to break up the calm water and then to take off across the wake. The pilot can then lift-off with minimal opposing suction force.

In the case of the Walrus, the R.A.F. Air-Sea Rescue Aircraft, the more serious problem for the pilot, once he had landed in the Channel and picked up the downed fighter pilot, was to be able to take off again under the usually very stormy conditions. Although the strong winds would help take-off, the very high waves worked against getting the aircraft up to take-off speed. Flight is only possible as Orville and Wilbur Wright discovered, when sufficient lift force is generated under the wing surfaces to lift the aircraft into the air. The aircraft wings are fabricated so that the distance from the leading edge to the trailing edge along the underside of the wing is less than that along the top of the wing. As the aircraft moves across the water on its take-off run against the wind, the air flows over the underside so that it is rarefied and at a lower pressure than the air flowing under the wing, thus creating a strong upward lift force. The magnitude of the lift force is dependent upon the speed of the air flowing across the wing surfaces and, although the wind was definitely strong enough when the Channel was stormy, the size of the waves made it very difficult for the Walrus with its low engine power to obtain the required forward speed. After three or four attempts the pilot usually managed to bounce from wave top to wave top and finally vault into the air, but it was never a smooth procedure.

When we had a pilot down in the Channel and called "Mayday," we wanted the Walrus to commence rescue without delay, but it was up to the pilot of the Walrus to decide whether he could affect the rescue or whether it was going to be impossible for him to get off again. Many times, I am sure, the Walrus pilot knew that the waves were too high for him to land and get off again safely, but his compassion for the downed pilot forced him to try, for which we were very grateful. One time only, I remember the operation was not too successful and both the downed pilot and the Walrus pilot had to wait for a Royal Navy motor torpedo boat squadron to rescue them. The Walrus was badly damaged after hitting a giant wave during the Walrus pilot's final attempt to take off.

By early 1944, we were having more and more difficulty replacing lost Mustang aircraft to keep up with squadron operations. The U.S. Air Force needed them for their own operations to escort B17 Flying Fortresses on their daylight bombing raids to Berlin. As a result, we were to be equipped with Hawker Typhoons.

We were advised that over the next few months, all pilots would have to build up their hours on Typhoons so that a smooth conversion from Mustangs to Typhoons would occur. In between flying operations on Mustangs, I began to fly Typhoons to search out any and all differences so that I would not have surprises while flying operationally.

The Typhoon's air speed at low level was about the same as the Mustang, but the comparison was all downhill from there. We were advised that, before starting the engine, the pilot should put on his oxygen mask and breathe oxygen at a level equivalent that required at 15,000 feet. Apparently, the cockpit filled with carbon monoxide from the exhaust. The first squadron to convert to Typhoons had to find this out the hard way by losing a pilot who crashed after passing out from the exhaust fumes. Luckily we were forewarned.

My test flights on the Typhoon also discovered that the aircraft had a serious aerodynamic design fault that made it unstable. It was probably due to lack of sufficient wing dihedral, or rudder fin surface, or both. As I flew along at low level, the aircraft would skid or slip sideways and would continue for fair distances without stabilizing and flying straight. I had to apply the rudder to straighten out each time. This meant that accurate navigation and cannon firing was going to be very difficult.

Another design fault was that the pilot had difficulty seeing behind him—a must for air operations—so that a rear-view mirror had to be mounted. I pressed on with my test flying regardless, because I knew that I had to eventually convert to Typhoons, but I resolved to fly most of my missions on Mustangs as long as one was available. I was flying the C.O.'s Mustang when I was shot down.

The Hawker Typhoon.
Source: *An Illustrated History of the R.A.F.* ©1990 Colour Library Books Ltd., Keystone Collection

Most of our sorties over Europe were extreme range for the aircraft so that fuel conversion was a must to ensure that we would be able to get back to our base. As a result we would fly at fast, but economical cruising speed with the propeller pitch lever set at coarse, the fuel mixture lever at lean, and the throttle lever pushed forward to produce 350 m.p.h. This would be comparable to driving a sports car in fifth gear or overdrive. Suddenly stepping on the accelerator would produce minimal acceleration, unless and until you also changed to a lower gear and allowed the automatic choke to enrich the fuel mixture in order to utilize the engine horsepower.

When jumped by enemy fighters, my left hand, with my wristwatch on the outside of my wrist, would flash to the throttle quadrant to, as quickly as possible, push all three levers fully forward to obtain fine pitch on the propeller, fully rich fuel mixture and a wide open throttle to produce maximum acceleration, torque and engine horsepower. This would be a short term setting until the emergency was taken care of when I would drop back to fast cruising speed again.

The problem was that my hand moved so quickly to the levers—I was grateful for my short reaction time—that the crystal on my wristwatch took a real beating. After a few operations, there were so many cracks in the watch crystal that I had difficulty reading the time. Since my navigation was based on precise timing, the problem became serious.

It appeared that the crystal was being cracked by grazing the heavy throttle quadrant each time my left hand flashed forward. By the time I had smartened up and turned the watch around to the inside of my wrist, a chunk of the crystal had fallen out. I had the crystal replaced and had no further problems. Obviously, the thickness of the watch itself was critical. To this day, I still wear my watch on the inside of my left wrist instead of the outside in contrast to probably 99.9% of the population.

Since our squadron, besides flying low level photographic missions, also flew high level missions, all pilots who were capable had to obtain a high altitude rating by passing a test course comprising eight hours in a decompression chamber simulating flying at 37,000 feet.

The decompression chamber was a large six-foot diameter steel tank—about ten feet long with benches along each side inside the tank to accommodate six pilots—three on either side—with oxygen masks and supply valve controls at each position. At one end of the tank was a large hinged entry door or hatch with an observation window in it which could be closed so that it would be airtight. An electric motor-driven air compressor was used to pump the air out of the tank once the pilots were in position and the door locked.

I remember it took the air compressor about an hour to pump the air out of the tank so that the air pressure would be equal to pressure at 37,000 feet altitude. We could communicate with the doctor overseeing the test. Course time did not begin until we got to the air pressure of 37,000 feet. Climbing up to altitude did not count. We found it really annoying when after taking an hour to achieve the high altitude pressure, one of the pilots would start moaning and groaning in pain and the doctor would order a descent which would take another hour. We would carry the complaining pilot out, close the door and start another hour-long ascent. It took a long time to complete the eight-hour at high altitude test requirement. At lighter than atmospheric air pressure, and particularly at the rarefied air pressure of 37,000 feet, nitrogen would leave the blood stream and settle in a gaseous state in the stomach and in the joints, sometimes causing intense pain in some people. We were taught not to make sudden moves or overstress unnecessarily at high altitudes to prevent this.

Eventually we were simulating cruising at 37,000 feet, at which point the doctor would have each one of us experience the effect of loss of oxygen by having our masks removed for a short time. Each pilot, in turn, would lapse into unconsciousness for a minute until the mask was replaced.

It was a long and drawn out course, so to add some spice to the event, when I removed Bill Irwin's mask and he passed out, Frank Jenkins removed Bill's left shoe and sock. When Bill woke up again after I'd replaced his mask, Frank and I told him that he'd removed his footwear himself before he passed out. The doctor had already told us that an oxygen starved brain caused pilots to do many strange things—if they were lucky, they'd regain consciousness and pull out of the dive before they crashed. I am not sure if Bill realized that we were kidding, but I hope so. He went missing within the month, believed to be killed off the Jersey Channel Island.

Although I passed the high altitude course and ran a few missions, I did not really like this type of flying. Taking vertical photographs at high level gave me the feeling of being stationary and although I could see just about the whole of Europe, it was quite boring. If I saw a flight of enemy planes trying to climb up to intercept me, I would simply alter course 5° or so, and I would leave them miles behind, hanging in the sky.

There was one other test that each pilot on the squadron had to take so as not to eliminate any flying options—the night vision test. The retina of the human eye utilizes cones for daylight vision and rods for night vision—both operate independently from one another. A pilot's perfect daylight vision had no bearing on his night vision and it had to be tested separately.

The test involved sitting in a pitch-black room, observing very faint silhouettes of aircraft, both enemy and friendly, flitting across an illuminated screen. I found that the only way I could identify the silhouettes of the enemy aircraft, which would appear for perhaps a hundredth of a second, was to not look at them directly, but rather out of the corner of my eyes. In practice, this is all one could do to identify aircraft at night.

I managed to get an above average rating, but other than the odd Night Ranger, I didn't do much night flying and I preferred low level flying during daylight hours.

7. Big Wing vs Low Level Line Abreast Battle Formation

Air Vice Marshall Leigh-Mallory and Wing Commander Douglas Bader of R.A.F. Fighter Command believed in what they called the, "Big Wing." This involved about 500 Spitfires from many squadrons in close V formation. The idea was to form up over England, then sweep across France, Belgium and Holland, engaging all the enemy fighters it encountered. In this way, they were sure that Germany's fighter force could be destroyed quickly. The *Luftwaffe* was not noted for stupidity, and was not about to waste its strength fighting such a force for no gain. As a result, they kept their aircraft on the ground while the, "Big Wing" flew over, and sent them up to attack the bombers and the reconnaissance aircraft when they came over. I can remember reading the newspaper headlines predicting the imminent demise of the German Air Force after being jumped by hordes of enemy fighters on every mission. In spite of the, "Big Wing," the enemy fighter force was a factor right to the end.

The "Big Wing" was a very unwieldy battle formation, slow to form up, and cumbersome to manoeuvre over enemy territory. The best they could do was slow turns, with the pilots, of necessity, paying more attention to maintaining their position in the formation than watching the enemy.

The line abreast formation, with 400 feet spacing and aircraft pairing up to become complete battle units, was far superior for us. In order to penetrate highly defended targets, get our pictures and get back with them, it was necessary to be as invisible to the enemy as possible. We therefore, flew all our missions at zero feet where radar could not pick us up. We could, however, be spotted by people in their observer towers as we flew by. To nullify this, we never flew directly to a target, but changed course frequently to make sure that if the enemy tried to guide aircraft to intercept us, it would be based on very erroneous information. This meant that our flight plans would have to be very accurate based on the latest wind speed and direction information, exact number of minutes and seconds of each leg of each course and very accurate flying and turns.

A pair of Mustangs, for instance, No. 1—the leader, and his No. 2, flying over France at zero feet and in 400 feet line-abreast spacing, would arrive at a point in the flight plan, where a 90° turn to the left was called for. Without any signal being required—radio silence was a must, except for emergencies—the No. 1 aircraft would rise to about 100 feet or so, and immediately make a steep turn to the left on to exactly the new course recorded. The No. 2 aircraft, if he was flying on the left of his No. 1, would also turn left under his No. 1, but more shallowly, so that he positioned himself at 400 feet spacing, but to the right of his No. 1. If he was flying on the right of his No. 1, then he would turn very steeply and climb so that he would fly over his No. 1 and line up on his left, once again at the 400 foot spacing. As soon as the turn had been completed, which would only take seconds at 400 m.p.h., they would drop down to zero feet as before and continue on the new course.

All of these manoeuvres were done very quickly at cruising speed, and if an enemy radar operator noticed anything at all, it would be a short blip while the aircraft were flying at 100 feet. We were sure the Germans weren't likely to be able to compute our final destination from these odd blips. As a result, when we arrived at the target, we invariably were not expected. This was the main reason that we were usually successful in getting back in one piece. The object was to arrive exactly at the target in spite of flying across France and into Germany, having to make perhaps five or six course changes, which, if you weren't careful, could cause many errors with sloppy turns, which would cumulate and you could end up far from the target. Searching around for the target was a NO! NO!

Since wind information was not that reliable and changed frequently, I always used the first leg of the flight, from base to the English coast, to check the accuracy of my flight plan and any error would be corrected for all remaining legs of the flight. When and if navigation was done carefully, we would see the startled look on the German's faces as we'd roar past the target and activate the camera, and we'd be turning to set course for home before they could get the guns trained on us. If they were really fast, we would see the flak exploding behind our tail.

This battle formation and method of quickly changing course was used to manoeuvre two to nine aircraft at zero altitude and at high speed in our operations in Europe. The leader, of course, had to rise up higher for the larger formations in order to allow the aircraft on the inside of the turn to safely pass beneath him.

I have purposely tried not to dwell on the aircraft and pilots that were frequently lost as a result of our squadron operations. I think that it will be understood that it was our contribution to the overall cost of defeating Hitler to maintain our Canadian way of life. Make no mistake, no one in Canada would want to live in accordance with his plan for the world, and his plan was for the next thousand years. Suffice to say that after one year on the squadron, I had survived and was a young veteran, and after two years, I was considered an old veteran—all of twenty-five years old.

8. Early Operations

The squadron comprised of two operational flights, "A" and "B", with a third, "C" for training. Pilots trained in "C" flight until they were needed to replace lost pilots in the two operational flights. I joined the squadron with two very good friends, who I had been with during our year-long training—Bill Irwin and Frank Jenkins. Bill and I had been moved out of "C" flight, Bill to "B" and myself to "A" flight, and had been flying on operations for about a month when he went missing, believed killed. He and his No. 2 had been on a mission to observe *Luftwaffe* activity on the many coastal bases. We called it the "milk run." This was early in the game before we preferred to strafe them not just observe.

Bill was to landfall near the Port of St. Malo in France just past the Channel Islands. This particular morning the English Channel was dead calm with no ripples on the surface of the water. It was also foggy, especially close to the Islands. As Bill flew past the Island of Jersey he apparently could not tell where the fog ended and the surface of the water started. In any case, he flew right into the water as if it wasn't there. His No. 2 told us later that he almost hit the water, too, but managed to pull up in time. Had Bill been flying almost any other plane but a Mustang, it would have floated for a few seconds, and he could have had a chance to get out, but the Mustang disappeared immediately.

This had a stunning effect on Frank and me. Bill had barely started on operations and the enemy had had really nothing to do with his death. The cause we concluded was pilot error. There were a tremendous number of flying accidents occurring everywhere at this time in the Operational Squadrons and in training.

At St. Hubert Service Flying Training School where I had trained, we were up doing night flying practice, when a heavy fog drifted in and engulfed the aerodrome. I was up, noticed what was happening, and landed immediately, as did all of the students except one, a fellow named Guthrie. He flew around above us for the better part of an hour, and instead of taking the options open to him such as flying to a clearer patch of sky and landing at another aerodrome, Dorval for instance, or crash landing in a field, or bailing out by parachute—any one of these options would have saved his life—he preferred to simply fly around in a panic and finally crashed into a barn and was killed.

Frank and I decided that there were really no accidents in flying—only happenings which were caused by the pilot who either did something he shouldn't have done, or neglected to do something he should have done. All we had to do then, was to do everything right and make sure we did not make any mistakes. Enemy action was a different problem, but we felt better that we had separated the two. We decided that checking and double-checking everything we did would eliminate the so-called accidents so that we could concentrate on the enemy.

While at St. Hubert S.F.T.S., Alec Ince and I were severely criticized for practising head-on attacks in Harvards. We arranged to always pass on the right and became pretty good at it. The chief of flying was an ex-Battle of Briton pilot, otherwise we might have been in real trouble. He had us on the carpet and simply said, "Fine! But don't do it anymore." I used this flying manoeuvre many times on operations against superior odds, especially when I was alone. I always managed to disperse the enemy long enough to get away.

The Focke-Wulf pilots were not good at low flying, whereas we spent the whole time at zero feet. If chased, rather than rise up to fly over a high tension power line and be in the perfect spot to be shot down, I would fly under the wires. The enemy would have to fly over, in which case, he would lose me, or in some cases, one of the planes would manage to hit the cables. The resulting power failure must have been huge.

There was a young fellow in "A" flight squadron who seemed to be a fair pilot. I had taken him on a few operations and he performed well, but was very quiet. After a month or two I still had not talked to him at length. During a short break from flying, the commanding officer called a mess dinner. We all attended and afterwards we had the odd beer. Suddenly, the silent pilot came over and slapped me on the back, and was extremely talkative to his old friend—me. The fellow's name was Willie Wilson. He told me that he had attended public school and his father was a lord. Later on he even sang, "If you were the only girl in the world, and I were the only boy." Gad!! In the morning, I tried to discuss his antics of the night before but he was back to quiet.

A few days later, I was leading a formation of five aircraft including his, on a Rhubarb, over France. We had taken care of several aerodromes although most of the aircraft had been moved to more distant bases by now. We were crossing back over the French coast to return to base when Willie called me to advise that his engine was overheating and his oil pressure was dropping. Knowing how loath Willie was to say anything—unless he had had a beer or two—I knew that it must be really serious. I took the flight up to 4,000 feet in case Willie had to bail out, and advised him that he should throttle back to save his engine.

I was hoping that we could limp back to base, but it was not to be. He was not maintaining height at all and we were already below 3,000 feet. I advised him to bail out immediately. After a few seconds, I noticed the coupe top fly off, and he went over the side. The parachute opened immediately as he drifted down. The remainder of the flight circled at about 2,500 feet. I followed Willie and called Mayday for air-sea rescue. Willie floated down to the water, and from then on didn't do anything. The wind kept his parachute inflated so that he was dragged from wave to wave. The procedure was to turn the harness buckle and punch it to free yourself of the parachute about six feet above the water, so that you would be free to get into your dinghy. Willie had made no move to do anything. I flew in low to see if he was struggling with his equipment, but he appeared to be unconscious. We circled until the air-sea rescue seaplane arrived and picked up Willie. I never knew just what happened. Lord Wilson visited the squadron to speak to me, but I knew nothing more than what I had already reported. I was going to try to find out just why Willie died, but no one seemed to know. It was possible that when his aircraft was hit by flack back at the enemy bases, that he himself had been hit and had lost a lot of blood. This would explain his passing out and not being able to get out of his parachute. Although I asked if he had been hit personally when he reported his engine trouble, he might have just said, "no" because he was a "stiff-upper-lip" type. However, they found no evidence of this on his body.

During the early part of my life, although I liked to think that I lived according to fairly high principles, I never really had these principles challenged. In this wartime environment, particularly the pilot's environment, because of the solitary nature of each encounter with the enemy, the challenge occurred immediately and had to be dealt with.

Some pilots relied on a superstitious belief that if they wore a lucky scarf, or always flew a supposedly lucky aeroplane, that they would be kept safe from harm. I was not superstitious and would purposely walk under ladders and use the number 13 to counteract any thought of reliance on such things. Besides, imagine having to get airborne immediately and not being able to find your lucky rabbit's foot!

Other pilots looked to religion to somehow protect them. I never felt self-centered enough to pray to God to favour me in my encounters with the equally deserving enemy pilots. I attended a few of the airfield church services to see if they had any answers as to how to win the war in a Christian way, but I found that they provided no leadership at all. They were preaching "Thou shalt not kill" with a "business-as-usual" attitude, war or no war, which, when I contemplated the four 20mm. cannons on my aircraft, made no sense at all. Obviously I did not have the luxury of living by these old rules. The danger in using a crutch to lean on, either superstitious or religious, was that you would tend to not strive as hard in everything you did since you believed that your crutch would always be there to take up the slack and protect you from harm.

Still other pilots were fatalists, believing that everything was pre-determined and was going to happen in a certain way regardless of what they did. This would result in the pilots doing less and less to help themselves since they were convinced that they could not change the inevitable result.

In the end, the philosophy for survival I chose to follow was to put the responsibility completely on myself where it belonged. It involved me doing everything possible to correct a problem by thinking fast and furiously to save myself, including pursuing the most unorthodox measures, exhausting all avenues available, and when this was done, but not before, to leave the final outcome to fate. Later, when my aircraft was shot down, I did just that, proving that the philosophy worked.

You don't have to live on this earth for very long to realize that God exists, and that the universe didn't just happen by accident. There is nothing accidental about the gene, nature's computer chip, which determines and regulates the characteristics of all of earth's species according to definite plans. A butterfly grows exactly as that species of butterfly has grown for millions of years, and when grown will go off and do butterfly things without further guidance. There is nothing accidental or random about the physical laws of the universe either. The laws of motion are not one value on Monday and another on Friday. They can be relied upon to be constant. As a result everything physical in the universe is mathematically predictable as to relative position therein.

It is true that modern scientific thinking believes in the big bang theory where all of the celestial bodies of the universe are moving out from the centre of an explosion at the speed of light—186,000 miles per second—but since all of the bodies are moving out at the same speed, their relative position to one another does not change, and the universe can be considered static even though distance is vast and measured in light years.

After only a few operations over enemy territory I was advised by Alec Brees, flight commander of "A" flight, that I would be flying as his No. 2 on a Rhubarb that he had planned for the next morning. We would be attacking enemy airfields in Northern France and Belgium, and any trains, truck convoys and other vehicles that we encountered in our sweep to help reduce the enemy's war capability. There would be five Mustangs flying line abreast at 400 feet spacing, making for an attacking force comprising twenty 20mm. cannons directed against the enemy's equipment in a giant 1,600-foot wide swath.

We took off and flew over Gravesend where Alec called for a few 90° low level turns, so that our skills would be at their peak when we arrived in France. We often used Gravesend, a small town east of London located on a bend in the Thames River, as a rendezvous point and general landmark for our squadron activities. At the time I did not think anything of it, but upon reflection now, it is rather a morbid and downbeat sounding place to use as the starting point from which to launch operations you hoped would be successful.

Satisfied that the flight was a skilled working team, Alex headed out over the Channel where he planned to landfall just south of Le Havre on the French coast. We always crossed the Channel at zero feet and at reduced airspeed to save fuel and hence increase our range. The reduced air speed, sometimes down as low as 200 m.p.h., caused the engine temperature to drop drastically, which could be dangerous if the engine quit so low down on the water. To guard against this happening, we had to periodically rise to 200 feet or so and increase speed to keep the temperature at a safe level. As we rose up, we would hear the "wow-wow-wow" sound of the enemy radar frequency beating with our VHF radio signal frequency and we knew that we were appearing on their radar screens. As soon as we could, we would get back down again, so that we could not be plotted. When we crossed the French coast at Le Havre our formation was a little ragged because of the evasive action we had to take to counter the heavy flak. No one was hit and we were soon heading inland low down again, above the trees, and in proper formation.

Almost immediately, Alec made a course correction to the left. He rose in the air and turned right into me. I turned left too, but I knew that I had to leave room for the Mustang on my left to also pass under Alec, so that I had to keep my wing tip just under Alec's to ensure that there would be enough room between me and the tops of the trees to accommodate him. It appeared very close, but we were soon at zero feet again and crossing over the boundary fence of a German airfield a few miles from the coast.

Alec had changed course so that our formation could fly right across the centre of the airfield. Each pilot engaged targets in front of him so that the formation would be maintained. I noticed Alec opening up with cannons on several FW 190s. One was taking off and was brought down after a short burst. I was able to strafe an FW 190 and a JU 88, which was being refueled. Unfortunately, being rather inexperienced, I aimed a little too high. A few of the shells hit the aircraft, but most hit the petrol bowser. Why it did not explode immediately, I do not know. I was very thankful that it didn't as I had to fly directly over it a split second later. The Mustang on my left must have hit a fuel dump with his cannon shells as there was a tremendous explosion, which lifted him violently to the right and he almost hit me. In no time, it seemed, we passed over the far airfield fence. There had been some flak from the enemy gunners, but we had surprised them, so that it was ineffective. As we continued flying north at zero feet, Alec alerted us to a train which was crossing in front of us, and advised that he would be attacking the engine. It was a really long train and streamed black smoke behind it as it struggled up a long slope. Alec attacked the engine and we all poured shells into the carriages as they came into range. The engine boiler blew up in a cloud of smoke and rusty steam, and I had to make way for Alec as he veered towards me, so that he would not have to fly through the debris. Everything seemed to be happening at once. While Alec was moving over towards me, I noticed that the Mustang on my left was in a violent flat turn away from me. At first I wondered why he would do this, but I quickly realized that while he had been firing at the train carriages, the cannons on the right wing must have jammed and ceased firing. The shell feed mechanisms to the cannon breaches were of good design and almost never jammed, even under very violent manoeuvres. Being blasted so violently sideways as he'd been back at the airfield, however, was probably too much for the mechanism on his right wing cannons.

When all four cannons are fired, the opposing recoil force causes a considerable decrease in air speed, but it is evenhanded. If the right wing pair of cannons jam and do not fire while the left wing cannons continue to fire, then the left wing will slow, and the right wing will not, and a violent flat veer to the left will occur, and the pilot will have to cease firing. There is nothing the pilot can do to clear the jam. His aim will be so distorted that he should not use his guns for the remainder of the sortie.

As we flew on, we encountered a small truck convoy. As usual it speeded up hoping to escape. Alec took out the lead truck. I had a staff car in my gun site, so I just touched the firing button and hit the car's front end causing it to summersault into the ditch and down a ravine. I just hoped the driver was a nasty Storm Trooper and not an innocent Mademoiselle.

Alec had done all the navigation on this sortie, but I noticed that we were now well into Belgium. As I expected, Alec took us across another enemy airfield. This one was loaded with ME 109 fighters and a few Heinkel 111 bombers. I was pouring shells into a small group of ME 109s when suddenly my guns ceased firing. I was out of ammunition. The rate of fire was 600 shells per minute so it didn't take long to run out. Perhaps if I had fired in shorter bursts, more carefully aimed, rather than spraying each target so liberally, I would be still firing.

Alec stopped another train before also running out of ammunition, whereupon he lead us out over the North Sea to return to base.

Our method of airfield attack proved to be very good. We were able to inflict the maximum damage for the least cost in pilots and aeroplanes, in the shortest time. We were able to do this mainly because of the element of surprise. We would attack an airfield only after flying several miles at zero feet. It required excellent navigational planning, so that the attacking flight could be assured of being able to fly over the centre of the airfield without having to search around and perhaps have to make a last minute course change which would make them visible to the gunners. Diving down to attack was foolish. Tony Bird proved the folly of this when he was killed by enemy airfield gunners after diving down from 30,000 feet or so, where he had been escorting returning U.S. Flying Fortress Bombers.

Flying a course which would take us across the centre of the enemy airfield, we would suddenly fly over the boundary fence in line abreast formation, and get right down to the deck again. We were flying fast, 400-420 m.p.h., but certainly not at the speed of sound, which, depending on the atmospheric air pressure, was close to 750 m.p.h., but somehow, perhaps we were so close to the ground, the enemy never seemed to hear us coming. I proved this time after time, by observing the surprised look on their faces as I passed by at zero feet. Without surprise there is no way that we could fly the width of the airfield with all those guns firing and not be brought down.

The time the attacking force was over the airfield was less than 20 seconds, so that the gunners, when they finally spotted us, had to get to their posts, rotate the gun to aim at us, and finally fire, by which time we were probably disappearing over the far boundary fence.

Since the success of our squadron's sorties relied heavily on very accurate navigational planning and very accurate flying, we used to "swing" or calibrate our aircraft compass at least once a month. This involved the manhandling of the aeroplane by the ground crew, supervised by the pilot, so that it was heading along the various points on an aircraft dispersal pad.

The magnetic north is not exactly at the earth's true north. It is a few hundred miles south and even changes location, within a narrow band, over the centuries. The compass, which utilizes a small bar magnet to line up in the earth's magnetic field, points to the magnetic north and not true north. As a result, a correction called the angle of variation had to be applied to all courses.

The No. 1 pilot of a two-member Mustang team, or in this case, Alec, the No. 1 pilot of a five-member team, was responsible for all of the navigation. Each of the other pilots had a map of the countries to be flown over, with the track to be followed, so that he could get back to base in the event that he became separated from his leader. His main function however, was to maintain flight formation and support his leader. The leader computed all the magnetic courses to be flown, in accordance with the available wind speeds and directions, complete with leg times, to get to the selected targets. In addition to the small-scale country maps, the leader would carry large-scale maps of the countryside leading up to each target, showing landmarks more clearly which he could observe readily at 400 m.p.h. and at zero feet, to double check that he was on course, as he approached each target. As a result, he would end up with 5 or 6 or more individual maps which he piled on the floor beside his seat, so that he could grab the proper map as required. I used to number the maps very clearly, in case I had to make a violent manoeuvre, and the maps ended up dispersed around the cockpit. At 400 m.p.h., we soon flew off the large scale map and would have to continually be reaching down for the next one.

The Operational Squadrons in the United Kingdom utilized trainer aircraft such as Tiger Moths, Majisters or Miles Masters to ferry people between airfields, because the fighters were single seaters. The problem with this was that after flying Mustangs most pilots considered these aircraft more like toys than real aeroplanes, and so flew them in quite a carefree or even careless manner, forgetting that crashing in a Tiger Moth would result in the pilot being just as dead as crashing in a Mustang.

One day I was flying a Tiger Moth with a sergeant from the photographic section of our squadron on board. The sergeant had to spend a day with Group Headquarters, about twenty miles south of our base, and using the Tiger Moth was the most convenient way of getting him there. The sergeant had mentioned to me that he really liked flying and would enjoy a bit of low flying. Taking him at his word, soon after taking off, I dropped down to give him a taste of real low flying over the farmers' fields. Feeling that the Tiger Moth was a very simple aircraft, not requiring all that much in flying skills, I got down really low over a wheat field.

I was so low that the undercarriage, to which the landing wheels were attached, was below the top of the wheat. The pull of the wheat reduced the air speed and tipped the whole aircraft forward so that the propeller, churned up the wheat and caused the aeroplane to move lower into the wheat. I knew that a crash was imminent. I couldn't think of any fancy flying skill that would prevent the aircraft crashing, so I used brute strength on the joystick to force the tail down and the undercarriage up about the wings as a fulcrum, while pushing the throttle forward for full engine power. If I crashed now, it would be a really good one.

I had to pull the stick with all my strength right back into my body, and hold it there for some time before the undercarriage finally broke free, and the aircraft popped up to 500 feet or so. The aircraft had cut quite a swath through the wheat.

As I flew on, I made sure that I flew over, rather than through the fields of wheat. When I landed at Group Airfield, I climbed out of the cockpit to apologize to the sergeant for flying so stupidly, and scaring him to death, but he was aglow with excitement and thanked me for the lowest flying experience that he had ever had. Of course it was. It was the lowest for me too, and I did not intend to repeat it, ever. Non-flying types never seemed to know when they should, or should not, be frightened.

9. An Interesting Leave

Lady Rider, a titled member of the aristocracy in Britain, had arranged for many of her friends to invite members of the aircrews of the various air forces, operating in Britain, to their homes for a week or so to be treated to the hospitality of a very grateful people. We decided that we would take advantage of the invitation. We contacted Lady Rider and she arranged for the three of us, Bill Irwin, Frank Jenkins and me to visit Mr. and Mrs. McGlaglon in Dumfries, Scotland. She told us that the McGlaglons owned a beautiful estate just across the English-Scottish border where they had many acres of forest and a lake full of trout on top of a mountain.

It sounded great to us, so we headed for Dumfries early the next day by train. We were picked up at the railway station in the village of Dumfries by Winchester, the McGlaglons' gamekeeper/chauffeur in a Bentley and driven to the McGlaglon estate. We met Mr. and Mrs. McGlaglon and their teenaged son and daughter. The teenagers were very well educated and appeared to know more about Canada than we did. During the day, we would be with Winchester, either tramping through the forest or fishing in the lake on top of the mountain. We caught some of the rainbow trout in the ice-cold water in the lake and Winchester brought them back to the cook for dinner

Winchester was a bit of a problem. He liked to drink and always wanted us to join him at the village pub before getting back to the estate. One day we made the mistake of going with him for a beer or two before joining the McGlaglons for tea.

Although there was plenty of liquor around the estate and Mr. McGlaglon enjoyed a drink in the evening, or whenever, no one drank too much, ever, and one obviously was expected to be under control at all times. As I sat down to have tea with the family this day, I really wished that we had not stopped off at the pub with

Winchester. I really did not like drinking this early in the day. Certainly being slightly high at tea time was not the way I liked to live.

I joined the conversation around the table with the McGlaglons and was very careful to speak as normally as I could. Mr. McGlaglon didn't seem to realize that he had an old soak for a gamekeeper. I passed the butter dish to Bill at his request and was startled to see him cut off a huge piece and place it on his plate. Butter was almost unheard of to us on R.A.F. stations, but I didn't think he liked it that much. Bill's action was noticed by Mr. McGlaglon, I think, but his face did not show it. I looked at Frank and it was obvious that he had definitely noticed what Bill had done as he was trying not to laugh. When I saw Frank trying not to laugh, I immediately saw the humour too, and this, together with the effect of the beer, which somehow makes anything and everything really hilarious, forced me to suppress my own laughter. We found out later that Bill had thought that it was cheese, not butter. By this time Bill had placed what he thought was cheese on his toast and had bitten into it. The look on his face when he realized it was butter, almost made me go into hysterics, but, of course, I couldn't so I bit my lip, coughed, and covered my mouth with the very fancy table napkin and managed not to choke. I couldn't stop laughing inside, but tried to remain silent, calm and collected on the outside.

Meantime, the son and daughter kept asking us every kind of question about almost anything so that we had to field these highly intelligent questions in the face of desperately trying not to laugh. I believe these two knew more about the Royal Air Force than we did. It was unbelievable.

The danger of bursting out laughing did not abate as Bill, now that he knew the mistake he had made with the most scarce and prized item in the United Kingdom, was determined to rectify the problem. He slid the butter onto his knife and I just knew that he was going to add insult to injury by trying to slip it back onto the butter dish. The butter dish was across the table in front of me, thank goodness, and I was not about to pass it over to Bill so that he could shock the McGlaglons a second time.

That was a very long tea, but eventually it was over, and we could retire to our rooms to recover. The McGlaglons, being kindly people, did not hold these shambles against us, and indeed, like true aristocrats, actually appeared to have forgotten it completely. We only hoped that they didn't think the obvious—what can you expect from colonial barbarians from Canada? They were very gracious in bidding us good-bye as we thanked them for a truly wonderful time. Winchester drove us to the railway station and didn't suggest we stop for a farewell beer. Had he done so, I am sure that he would have been bodily booted out of the car.

Strangely, we never again took advantage of Lady Rider's hospitality. We seemed to be always too busy for anything but a few days at a time away from flying.

10. London Air Raids

Lower ranks and non-commissioned officers received their pay, weekly, in cash from the Squadron Paymaster during pay parade. Commissioned officers, on the other hand, had their pay deposited into a bank of their choice once every month. My bank in Canada was the Dominion Bank of Canada at the corner of Bay and King Streets in Toronto, so when I was posted overseas, I opened a temporary account with the Dominion Bank in London, since I did not know just where I would finally be located. As it turned out, I was on many different R.A.F. airfields in southern England, but all fairly close to London, so that I was able to make my account permanent. I didn't get to London very often, so it was a great way to save money.

In any case, there wasn't much need for actual cash on the squadron. We didn't do much more than fly, and anything that cost money, such as the mess bill, was handled on the British "never-never" plan, and paid at the end of each month. I would take the train to London once a month, when I could spare the time, to check the account and pick up the necessary cash.

On one of these trips to my London bank, I stepped out of the taxi at the corner of Threadneedle and Bank Streets where my bank was located, and was shocked to find that it had disappeared, along with several of the buildings which had been next door. I looked across the street to confirm that St. Paul's Cathedral was there, so the taxi driver had let me off at the correct street corner, all right.

The *Luftwaffe* had obviously visited one night during the past month. I did not know when the bank was destroyed, but it must have been at least a week past as most of the rubble had been cleaned up. The cathedral had not been hit.

Those Germans, not satisfied with trying to knock me out of the sky every time I flew over the continent, were now trying to ruin me financially. I figured that with the bank destroyed, I had lost my life's savings, at least tuppence-hapenny anyway.

Upon closer examination of the bombed-out site, I realized that I had forgotten about the "never-give-up" character of the British people. I walked down a flight of patched-up cement steps, opened a battered steel door, and found the bank staff carrying on business as usual in the basement. Since this was the financial district of London, no one had been there during the nighttime hours when the enemy bombers came over, so no one was killed or hurt.

They advised me that I was not penniless as I had feared, and if anything, they appeared surprised at my concern for their safety. I guess you can get used to anything.

Throughout 1942 and well into 1943, the *Luftwaffe* carried on their night bombing attacks against London. From our various bases close to London, we could hear the anti-aircraft gunfire, the dull roar of the bombers' engines, and see the powerful beams of light from the many searchlights scanning the sky to pick up the attackers so that the gunners could bring them down. Every now and then, success would be indicated by a brilliant flash in the sky, followed by something falling to earth in flames.

When in London during these nighttime air-raids, we always felt that it was our duty to act like officers and gentlemen to provide a good example to the people. As a result, we never used any of the air-raid shelters. The people really respected us, so that we did not think it appropriate to rush to the shelters when the air-raid siren sounded and take a seat away from some local person. We preferred to carry on doing what we had planned and pretty well ignored the air-raids. My personal attitude was that the bombs were not being aimed at me, so that I really wasn't too concerned, in contrast to the flak encountered when I flew over the continent, which definitely was. Normally the subways and the buses continued to operate unless sustaining a direct hit.

This night we were on our way back to our base at R.A.F. Odiham, after a quick visit to London. We planned to walk to the nearest underground station, take the subway to Waterloo Railway Station, and then the train to Basingstoke, and walk the half mile to the base. The air-raid was at its peak as we walked along the street on our way to the underground station. We were almost hit, not by bomb fragments or other debris, but by dozens of shell casings which were dropping down from the roof of a building where a big gun was firing furiously at the attacking enemy bombers. The shell casings were being ejected from the breach of the gun each time a shell was fired. The casings were made of good quality brass or bronze, and clanged and rang very loudly as they bounced in front of us on the sidewalk. I suppose the gun crew did not expect people to be walking along the sidewalk during the air-raid. We continued on our way, staying close-in to the building and managed to keep out of the way of the flying shell casings.

We finally made it safely to the underground entrance and hurried down the stairs to the platform to await the next train to Waterloo. As we walked farther along the platform, we were very careful not to step on the dozens of people who were lying on blankets in a row all along the length of the platform, fast asleep in their nightclothes. These people were either using the subway as their air-raid shelter, or they had been bombed out of their homes and had nowhere else to live. There were people like these sleeping in all of London's underground stations. We tried to speak softly so that we would not awaken anyone, especially the children. We needn't have bothered though. When the train finally came rushing in to the station, with its brakes screeching in the effort to come to a stop, all of the sleeping people were oblivious to the commotion. When we boarded the surface train at Waterloo Station, the air-raid was still raging, but the remainder of the journey to our base was uneventful.

Throughout the bombardment, St. Paul's Cathedral was never hit and Buckingham Palace, a much larger structure, had only minor damage. I am quite sure that these two buildings were not spared by any kind feelings on Hitler's part. On the contrary I would guarantee that he demanded that both be destroyed, as the British morale would have been undoubtedly devastated.

To my thinking, not being an expert on bombing, but appreciating the "anything-but-exact-scientific-nature" of the art, the reason that these buildings were never hit was the very fact that they were aimed at. The enemy bomb commanders knew that they were priority targets, and as a result, the law of probabilities, together with the many unknown variables—wind speed and sheer differences between bombing height and ground level—for which no bomb sight then, or even now, could possibly compensate for, made certain that they would not be hit. They would be close though. Aiming at St. Paul's for instance, probably resulted in hitting my bank just across the street. Perhaps the Germans would have had more success if they had deliberately aimed off-target by a street width or so. Who knows! Ignoring the heavy flak from London's many guns defending the city, and flying dead straight and level throughout the bombing run would provide a stable platform from which the bombs could be dropped, is really all enemy crews could do. The unknown external wind forces acting on the falling bombs always managed to deflect them from their intended target. I suppose that plus or minus thirty feet, after falling thirty thousand feet, is not really bad, but in this business, it always changed a hit into a miss.

Somewhat similar problems existed in hitting targets in air-to-air or, air-to-ground firing, using wing-mounted cannons or machine guns. But error correction was at least in the hands of the pilot, and once the physical laws were understood, good accuracy could be routinely achieved.

To illustrate this, early in my first operational tour when I was young and comparatively inexperienced, I was sent with my No. 2 on a sortie to attack marine traffic on the Seine River in France. Leaving England at Beachy Head, we crossed the channel and made landfall in France at the Somme Estuary while keeping away from the port at Le Havre, which was very heavily defended. The Seine River emptied into the English Channel at this point.

Flying at low level and at high cruising speed, 380 to 400 m.p.h., I proceeded to follow the river in the direction of Paris while keeping an eye out for enemy shipping. My No. 2 provided top cover. Since the river did not flow in a straight line, but wandered back and forth across the landscape like a giant snake, I was forced to do very steep turns when my wings were just about vertical, first to the right and then completely over to the left, in order to follow the river's contours. As I continued on, I noticed a large river barge and opened up with all four cannons. Although the barge filled my gun sight ring, I didn't appear to be scoring any hits. Farther up the river I came upon another barge around another bend in the river, and once again, with the target filling my ring sight, gave it a burst and once again, appeared to be hitting nothing. I did notice that the cattle in the fields on both sides of the river, which had been quietly grazing, were now widely dispersed and scrambling to get over the hedge fences. Obviously I had been a little off target. The cannon shells were ending up everywhere, but on the target. With the cannons mounted on the wings and having to throw the aircraft around so wildly to follow the river, meant that the individual shells were leaving the cannon muzzles with all sorts of weird forces acting on them. Their resulting trajectories and striking points would have no relationship to that aimed at by the ring sight. From my observations, it appeared that the target aimed at was the one point where no shells were impacting. Since I was getting absolutely nowhere with this method, I advised my No. 2 that I was aborting the attack. I stopped following the river and flew a short distance away to think about it. I reasoned that longitudinal attack was impossible and that an attack ninety degrees to the river, and to the direction the barge was moving, was the only alternative. I headed back to the river, planning to cross over at right angles and looked for German-manned barges. I was at zero feet, flying straight and level while maintaining stable control and constant speed and keeping the barge in the center of my gun sight. This effectively eliminated all those forces, which had been distorting my aim earlier. When in range, I pulled the trigger, and was relieved to see many strikes on the barge hull. I flew on over the river for a mile or so, turned around and came back to the river to attack another barge with excellent results.

I returned to base, with my No. 2, feeling that I had really learned something, but also wondering why it was that I always seemed to have to do it the hard way. I decided I would never again bother to fire my guns without first eliminating all the extraneous forces, and establishing the necessary stable gun platform.

11. Weakness of the Aircraft

After Bill Irwin proved, what we had been told, that a Mustang cannot be successfully ditched, I thought that I would find out for myself the truth to the other so-called weakness of the aircraft—that it was impossible to control at low speeds, particularly at low level. The Americans had had many crashes apparently. Since our squadron spent all of its time flying at low level, I figured I better know for sure. I booked in for an hour of aerobatics, took off and climbed to 30,000 feet to have lots of room to experiment.

I had never stalled a Mustang. Unlike the Tiger-Moth and the Harvard, it had not been part of the training. I wondered why, and wanted to find out. With all this distance between me and the ground, I slowly closed the throttle. While keeping the nose up and the wings level, I closed the throttle more and more—the speed dropped quickly. As the speed approached the stall, the aircraft began shuddering, which is normal. At about 78 m.p.h. though, the right wing dropped viciously and I hit my head on the coupe top as the aircraft flipped onto its back and headed straight down. The altimeter was spinning like a top and air speed was increasing at a fantastic rate.

A falling body, such as a pilot before he opens his parachute, drops at an acceleration rate of 32 feet per second, due to the force of gravity—according to our friend Sir Isaac Newton—up to a maximum velocity of 120 m.p.h. At this speed the acceleration drops to zero, and the gravity force is exactly equal to the opposing force of resistance to the air. This maximum speed is called terminal velocity. All diving or falling aircraft have a terminal velocity. A Tiger-Moth's is quite low, and even a Harvard's is reasonable, both falling to earth in flat spins.

The Mustang was obviously a different story. There was nothing flat about what it was doing. The speed was in excess of 700 m.p.h., and the altitude was below 6,000 feet by the time I decided that it was not going to reach its terminal velocity, and I pulled it out of the dive. The lack of air resistance was the reason it could fly so fast, so I couldn't have it both ways. With 700 m.p.h. or so on the clock, I headed up to 30,000 feet again, and hardly had to use the engine. It was just like a roller coaster. I spent the rest of the time experimenting and discovered that I needed a minimum of 8,000 feet to pull out of a stall. Diving away from an enemy aircraft would be a sure winner, if we were operating at 20,000 feet or higher. Since most missions were low level this would not be too useful, and I had to resolve to always keep my air speed well above stalling. But now I knew for sure. I had the answer and I could fly at zero feet without worrying.

12. Flying Strategies and Incidents

Although, when I joined the squadron I already had hundreds of training hours, I really learned to fly operationally under the direction of Alec Breeze, Flight Commander of "A" Flight and Tony Bird, Flight Commander of "B" Flight. They were both superb pilots. Practising ninety degree turns, flying low level in battle formation with these two gentlemen was something to remember. Flying in the No. 2 position, every time you looked up, there would be either Tony or Alec coming at you, so that you had to move fast to move under or over them to always stay in formation. Manoeuvring a Mustang about the leader, realizing the very complicated shape—two protruding wings and a tail attached to a fuselage, with a fourteen-foot diameter whirling propeller in front—within the very restricted space available, was not learned easily. This taught us to move quickly and aggressively, but not in a ham-fisted manner. Ham-fisted movements of the stick, although we were all strong enough to do it, would result in the destruction of the smooth flow of air across the elevator and/or the aileron control surface and control of the aeroplane would be lost. To regain control, the pilot would have to let go of the stick to allow smooth airflow over the control surfaces again, and then move the stick more gently. The secret was to control the aircraft just on the point of air turbulence over the control surfaces, but never to go over the edge, particularly when flying at low level, as there would probably be insufficient time or height to allow the pilot to recover.

This is rather incorrectly called a high-speed stall and can occur at any speed, including the aircraft's normal stalling speed, where loss of lift also occurs. If a pilot dives down at speed to attack a train, or whatever, and over-controls in pulling up so as to cause the smooth flow of air over the elevator control surfaces to be disturbed, the aircraft will not respond to the pull-out and will continue in the dive until it hits the train or the ground just as if the control action had not been made.

To fly always just short of this point, but very quickly and aggressively, so that the maximum manoeuvrability of the aircraft is obtained, was the objective of the training. Eventually our skills were honed to the level required and we were ready for operations.

Tony Bird, while being a superb pilot in the air, apparently relaxed too completely when he landed, as he had several taxiing accidents and chewed-up the tail of a Mustang which had landed ahead of him.

The normal resting attitude of a fighter aeroplane in those days with its very low tail wheel and high main wheels to ensure that the three-blade, fourteen-foot diameter propeller didn't strike the ground, was excellent for short landing runs when touch-downs were three-pointed, but taxiing was a real problem. The pilot could not see over the huge engine in front of him, but had to zigzag along the taxi strip, turning first left and then right to be able to see ahead at least part of the time. The responsibility of not hitting things while taxiing rests with the pilot. Although airfield organization was very good most of the time, emergencies did occur when non-procedural moves were made, such as towing a petrol bowser along a taxi strip or even across the main runway. Pilots always had to realize this and be on the alert. With Tony, his unfortunate accidents were pretty well overlooked in the face of his flying talents.

Tony had many friends in the U.S. Air Force, and in particular in Mustang Squadrons engaged in escorting B-17 Flying Fortresses on their daylight bombing missions to Berlin. Tony used to fly with his U.S. friends while he was on leave from our squadron. Unfortunately, returning from one such mission, he dived down to attack an aerodrome, somewhere in Germany, and was killed as the result of a direct hit by the airfield gunners on his fuel tank.

Returning from a four-aircraft photographic sortie deep into France one day, we were flying about 2,000 feet because of poor weather, when we were jumped by a flight of Focke-Wulf 190s. We immediately broke into the attacking enemy and then, because we had valuable photographs on board, we did a wing-over and dived for the deck. We all pulled out close to the ground to proceed at low level to the coast, except for one pilot who must have experienced a high-speed stall at pull out, as his aircraft mushed down to the ground until his propeller actually struck the ground damaging it and causing his engine to vibrate violently. He was forced to quickly throttle back to prevent the engine shaking itself to pieces. The maximum speed he could attain was about 120 m.p.h. The enemy aircraft were nowhere to be seen, so we formed a protective box around the disabled aircraft and headed for the coast.

Our progress was so painfully slow and I could see that we were really vulnerable if attacked, that I called the pilot of the damaged aircraft and advised that he should continue on course with his No. 2, while myself and my No. 2 would maintain high cruising speed in a criss-cross pattern above them providing protective top cover in case the 190s reappeared.

Seconds later, I noticed that they had reappeared about a mile away to our right. They had formed up again after following us down, and appeared to be flying parallel to us towards the coast. Because our speed was restricted to that of the disabled aircraft, the 190s had not yet spotted us and were soon a few miles short of the coast. They were obviously not aware of our damaged aircraft situation, where our forward speed was reduced to less than one third of normal cruising speed, and as a result, were searching for us miles ahead of our actual position. It was imperative that we keep as low a profile as possible if we were going to be able to slip by them without being spotted. I knew that, if we were attacked, or if the damaged Mustang engine failed—and there was no guarantee that it would keep running—then the pilot would have to bail out or crash land. I called the disabled aircraft pilot again and suggested that he alter course ten degrees to the right away from the searching 190s and drop down even lower. I did the same so that I was no longer top cover, but at the same height as the rest of the Mustangs. In this way I hoped that none of us would be visible to the enemy radar and we couldn't be seen visually on the horizon.

We eventually crossed the French coast. The disabled engine continued to run and as we dropped down to cross the channel, it appeared that we might make it back to England. There was no sign of the 190s and we could see the white cliffs at Beachy Head. They seemed so close, but at our reduced speed, it seemed to take us forever to make it.

As it was, the pilot, having to increase speed to clear the cliffs, and becoming alarmed at the increasingly violent engine vibrations, put his aircraft down on the first landing strip he saw after passing over Beachy Head.

We circled to make sure the pilot was not injured. He had made a good landing on the strip, and was soon out of the aircraft and waving to us. This landing strip was one of many along the coast that had been continually attacked by marauding enemy fighter bombers to the point where they were not being used and there were no facilities. We formed up and continued on to our base.

The squadron communication aircraft, a two-seater Miles Master—very similar to the Harvard—was dispatched to the strip to pick up the pilot and the camera film and to drop off the service police corporal who would guard the downed aircraft until the ground crew could get there.

Later on, upon examination, it was found that five of the six bolts holding the propeller to the propeller boss had sheared off and all of the power from the engine drive shaft had been transmitted to the propeller through the one remaining bolt. The Mustang was obviously a very rugged aeroplane, thank goodness.

13. Fighter-Bomber Affiliation

One other function the squadron was required to perform was "Fighter-Bomber Affiliation," to assist R.A.F. Bomber Command in their battle against the *Luftwaffe*. Bomber Command was losing too many of their heavy bombers; Lancasters, Halifaxes and Sterlings, to Germany's new Focke-Wulf 190 fighter and wanted to do something to reduce their losses. With the Mustang being the only R.A.F. fighter which was close in performance to the German fighter, we were selected to work with the various bomber squadrons to see if their performance could be improved. We were in almost daily contact with the Focke-Wulf squadrons and were well aware of their latest attack methods. Air Ministry requested that senior members of our squadron work with each of the various crews on the bomber squadrons over the next few months.

The training was to be done outside our normal scheduled flying duties. It was set up so that when we had a spare hour or so, we would rendezvous with a bomber at 25,000 feet or so, over a well-known landmark. When we arrived, we would fly up to the bomber, waggle our wings, and then commence our sequence of simulated attacks. I was never able to speak to the bomber pilot on the VHF. All it would have required was the installation of the proper frequency crystal in my set, but it never happened for some weird reason, and I always had to wait until we were on the ground to discuss anything.

Both my wing mounted cannons and the machine guns on the bomber would be in the "No Fire" position, however the Ciné Cameras, which would photograph everything aimed at, would be switched on, so that firing accuracy would be recorded on film.

We would run through all of the attack strategies that we knew the Focke-Wulf 190s were using against the bombers, attacks made from rear upper and lower, right and left, out of the sun, head-on from the front, and the most deadly of all, climbing up from ground level to attack the underbelly of the bomber where they had no lookout.

Unlike fighters, where the pilot had complete peripheral vision to spot enemy attacks, the bomber pilot had to rely on his crew to advise him on the intercom, just where the attack was being launched by the enemy fighter, and when he should take evasive action. The fighter's guns were harmonized to provide a firing pattern, some hundreds of yards ahead, which would be most effective in bringing down the bomber, and the pilot would not fire until he was sure that he was within this range. Fighters armed with wing-mounted machine guns had to be close to 300 yards or less from the bomber, to score hits, whereas the cannon-equipped Mustang and Focke-Wulf could commence firing at double this distance and still obtain good results.

The theory was for the bomber air gunner to quickly and accurately estimate the fighter's distance from the bomber as he came in to attack, and then call for the pilot to turn sharply in the direction from which the attack was coming. If the fighter was attacking from the left rear of the bomber, the gunner would wait until it was almost in range and about to fire. He would then advise his pilot to "break left," whereupon the pilot would turn steeply to the left. The bomber would be moved safely out of the enemy pilot's gun sight ring, and the cannon shells would roar harmlessly by. At this point the bomber gunner, who was equipped with multiple machine guns, would find that the enemy fighter was now in range of his guns, and he could direct his fire on the passing aircraft, usually quite effectively.

The affiliation always seemed to follow the same pattern. There was a very steep learning curve involved. The first session was pretty pitiful. The air gunners were always firing too soon, away out of range, and there was no problem for me to get in close with devastating results. Their evasive action was too timid and far too late, as the Ciné photos proved later. They developed all of the Ciné film, mine and the bomber's air gunners, and we had a screening of everything together with an explanation of what happened on each attack, and what should have been done to prevent me scoring hits.

When I made my attack on the belly of the bomber, by roaring up from ground level—the Focke-Wulf's favourite—the bomber pilot seemed to be obsessed with getting in my way, rather than evading. In the end, I was forced to do the evading. As I came up underneath the bomber to simulate the attack, my speed was greatly reduced, with the resulting loss of effective control. Each time I turned to avoid hitting him, the bomber pilot would move his aircraft right in front of me. He obviously couldn't see what he was doing, but I was in real danger of ramming him. This type of kamikaze evasive action was fine if you didn't mind going down with the enemy fighter, but it was certainly not recommended. I was now so close to the bomber that I was forced to close the throttle completely, and allow my aircraft to fall back in a complete stall. I had been on a fairly long mission earlier in the day—at 4:30 a.m. —and I felt rather tired now, and not really in the mood to wrestle with a stalled Mustang while falling 8,000 feet or so, before being able to pull out again. However, I am sure that the bomber crew were so confused by this time that they did not even notice my absence.

The second session with the same crew showed some improvement, indicating that they were moving up on the learning curve. Coordination of the pilot and crew always seemed to be the most difficult thing to learn. They had to operate as a team. Getting the bomber out of the fighter's line of fire at precisely the right time was the key to success, and it took practice.

By the third session, I was astounded at the difference. The pilot was obviously getting his "break" commands right at the crucial instant and was literally throwing the big bomber right or left as required. Just before I fired at the bomber with it filling my gun sight ring, it would be yanked to the left or right and my Ciné film would show me firing into space. In the deadly attack from ground level, I tried as hard as I could to keep the aircraft in my gun sight ring, but somehow the pilot managed to stand the giant Sterling bomber on its ear and escape. This was, of course, exactly what had to be done for the evasive action to be effective. Very aggressive action on all of the crew's part was necessary.

The Ciné film screening proved to be much different this time. The whole crew was in high spirits at their successes and now seemed to be confident in their ability to win against the real thing. I stayed for tea in the mess and afterwards was given a great send-off as I took off to return to base. Perhaps this would help them get through the war in one piece.

14. Night Ranger Sortie

I cannot remember the exact date, but sometime during January or February of 1943, we were engaged in daytime photographic sorties along the European coastline, low level sweeps against enemy aerodromes in Belgium and France, and we were also scheduled for Night Ranger sorties to keep the pressure on the enemy during darkness. The weather was particularly poor at that time of year for night-time sorties. A bright moon with little or no cloud was required. I had been standing by without success for a week or so, when the meteorological officer advised that this night was expected to be clear and moonlit over the continent. A Night Ranger sortie involved a low level patrol by a single Mustang sent over the continent to attack the enemy's night-time activities within the range of the aircraft.

I took off shortly after midnight and flew down to Beachy Head on the south coast of England where, after passing over the two-hundred-foot-high cliffs, I dropped down to just above the water to cross the channel and landfall at the Cherbourg peninsula. The moon was shining brightly and the weather seemed just about perfect. As I approached the peninsula, I climbed to cross the coast and tracer flak came up to meet me.

I took evasive action by "stirring the porridge," as we called it. This involved moving the joystick in a slow circle, either clockwise or counter-clockwise. Rotating in a clockwise direction, for instance, I would move the stick back to climb, then to the left to turn left, then forward to dive, then right to turn right, and finally back again to climb again. This caused the aircraft to take an extremely erratic path through the sky to confuse the enemy gunners. If the joystick moves were made carefully and symmetrically, the aircraft would end up on the original course and more or less at the same height, and the flak would have hit nothing. This was preferable to random evasive action where time was wasted afterwards getting back on course and/or living with the navigational errors.

I flew on inland at low level towards the Paris area, but found little or no enemy activity. As I flew on east of Paris, I was able to attack aircraft on the ground at two airfields with fair results though the flak was intense. I turned north towards the Dutch-German border and was able to attack a train and a truck convoy. As usual, the convoy tried to outrun me, which was always a mystery to me. Since I was doing 380 to 400 m.p.h. and the trucks, driving at night with no headlights, even with the bright moon, could get up to maybe 70 m.p.h. maximum, there was never any contest. If the convoy had simply stopped on the side of the road, perhaps under the trees, I probably would not have taken the time to do anymore than fire a few cannon shells into one or two of the trucks. At low level and 400 m.p.h. it is physically impossible to do more, unless I attacked from the side—which I did not have time for. As it was, with the convoy trying to outrun me, I was able to blast the whole convoy off the road and into the ditch. Well, actually, I stopped the lead truck, and the rest of the convoy, going wide open, either hit it or went off the road on their own.

As I flew on I noticed that in order to stay in the moonlight, I had to move farther and farther east. The clouds seemed to be building up fast to the west. I hadn't realized that the weather was deteriorating. Where was all that beautiful weather they promised me?

A weather front, comprised of cumulus nimbus storm clouds from ground level to at least 30,000 feet, appeared to be sweeping in from the west at surprising speed. I turned around and headed south to see if I could get under the front and back to the channel, but there didn't seem to be any openings. I was flying at about 4,000 feet, trying to find a break in the cloud wall, when I noticed a German aircraft a few hundred feet below and ahead of me, flying in the same direction. I recognized it as a Mark "K" Heinkel 111 bomber. This was the heavy bomber that Hitler sent against

England in earlier years, but was probably now being used to transport senior military staff to the Atlantic Defence Wall along the English Channel. General Rommel was in charge of this defence, so perhaps he was on board! Unfortunately, the Heinkel was not a fast aircraft so that no matter how I tried to slow up in preparation for attack, I was already ahead of the bomber and we were both going in and out of cloud. I realized that I would have to do a 360 degree turn and lose about a thousand feet of height to get into a position to shoot the aircraft down. I did not feel too confident of success, but I thought that I had to try since this type of encounter was the real reason for Night Rangers.

I did a quick wing-over right into the cloud wall and had to do the 360 degree turn on instruments. When I broke out of the cloud, I saw the bomber ahead of me within cannon range, but just entering the cloud bank, I just had time for a quick burst from my four cannons and scored a hit at the right wing root and engine before it disappeared into the cloud bank. I flew along the cloud wall waiting for the aircraft to emerge, but I realized after awhile, that it was probably heading directly to the channel and I would not see it again. In any case, whether or not it had sustained serious damage from my attack, it would no doubt prefer to stay within the safety of the cloud bank. So much for this sortie.

I was nearing the French-Spanish border now and I had not seen a break in the cloud to the west. The storm clouds appeared to be sweeping across the whole of Europe. This drastic weather change was not all that unusual at this time of year. Many such storms would roar in from the North Atlantic and engulf Britain and Europe without much notice. We couldn't wait for perfect weather if we were going to carry on our air operation effectively, but I had hoped that, as in the past, I would be able to get around or get under the weather to get back to base. It appeared that this time I would need help to get out of France, across the English Channel and to my base in southern England.

I switched the VHF radio to the emergency channel and called Fighter Control to request a "homing" to my base. A WAAF– Women's Auxiliary Air Force–at Fighter Control came on the air and I was astonished how young she sounded. At first I thought that a twelve- or thirteen-year-old had picked up the microphone, but then I realized that she would have to be at least eighteen years old to join the WAAFs. I did not feel at all confident having to put my life in this gal's hands, but I had no other choice. She requested that I climb to 5,000 feet to improve the weak signal she was receiving from me due to the weather and the distance, circle and transmit continuously. Although maintaining radio silence while over enemy territory was ingrained in my mind, I realized that this was an emergency. Control requested this action from me in order for the R.D.F.—Radio Direction Finding—station to pinpoint my exact location over Europe, so that they could guide me back to my base. I, therefore, quickly climbed to 5,000 feet and proceeded to circle away from the cloud bank, while counting slowly and deliberately into my helmet microphone.

The R.D.F. equipment employed a rotatable antenna which could be accurately aimed at the source of a VHF radio signal. The distance between stations, called the "baseline," had to be 150 to 200 miles for good accuracy. For instance, an R.D.F. station in southern England could work in conjunction with a station in Scotland to obtain good accuracy. I did not know the location of the R.D.F. stations as it was always on "a need to know" basis. They were available to me on the VHF emergency channel so it wasn't necessary for me to know, and the fewer people that knew the better their security. Each of the two R.D.F. stations could locate the signal on a line from their station to my aircraft, expressed as an angle to the baseline joining the two stations. Knowing the length of the baseline, and the two angles to this baseline, would describe the complete triangle. By plotting this data on the table map, the WAAF could compute the course to get me home. She interrupted my counting to advise me of the course to steer. I stopped circling and turned onto the course she had given to me. This led me straight into the cloud bank.

A quick look out the coupe top, ahead and down, confirmed that I was in ten-tenths cloud and would not likely see the ground again for some time. Clouds are rated from one-tenth, a few light fluffy clouds, through five-tenths—half cloud and half clear sky, all the way to ten-tenths—solid cloud, no clear sky. In addition to the ten-tenths cloud, it was night-time which meant that I couldn't even see my wings. There was no point in looking out of the cockpit at all. All of my flying from now on had to be done with reference to the cockpit instruments only.

Under clear skies, the pilot uses VFR—Visual Flying Regulations—to fly with reference to the natural horizon, which is the optical appearance of the earth and sky coming together some twenty miles distant in a horizontal line. With IFR—Instrument Flying Regulations—the pilot must use the artificial horizon and associated flight instruments to keep the wings level, maintain height and stay on course.

The artificial horizon is a thin black line within the instrument which is gyro-powered so that it remains horizontal relative to the earth, independent of aircraft attitude. Violent flight manoeuvres would, however, cause the gyro to topple so that the pilot would have nothing with which to compare aircraft attitude. This is why control movement had to be slow and deliberate when flying IFR.

When flying VFR, a small metal aeroplane attached to the frame of the instrument, depicting the actual aircraft, could be moved about the artificial horizon line with the use of the joystick, with reference to the natural horizon. The instrument was calibrated so that with the model aeroplane's wings level and the nose just touching the artificial horizon line, the aircraft would be flying straight and level. If the nose was below the horizon line, the aircraft would be in a dive; if above, it would be in a climb; if the left wing was down, the aircraft would be turning left; and if the right wing was down, it would indicate a right turn. Reference to the altimeter and the air speed indicator indicated the steepness of a dive or climb so that the pilot could adjust accordingly.

Most fighter pilots had no instrument flying training. They were taught VFR only. If they flew into cloud, they had to get out quickly if the cloud was ten-tenths, or run the risk of stalling and hitting the earth, or have to bail out. Because of our long range missions which could involve weather changes, we were given extensive instrument flying training, but we lacked practice and preferred to get back to base on our own, if we had the option. We only called Control under dire emergencies, such as now. Control response to fighter aircraft was very fast. When flying on instruments, abrupt control moves were avoided as overshooting would occur and cause erratic flying.

With the bomber, where control response was much slower, and usually employed automatic pilot equipment for long flights, it was not the same problem. I can remember flying an old Armstrong Whitworth Whitley, an early Second World War British bomber— I turned the control wheel to the left to do a left turn, and was amazed at how long I had to wait for the monster wing to drop and finally turn to the left. I then had to move the wheel past center and around to the right in order to stop the turn, and finally fly straight again.

With fighter aircraft, and in particular the Mustang, movement of the control stick and response of the aircraft was instantaneous. Shifting in my seat, or a few seconds of inattention, could result in a change in height, up or down, of a few hundred feet, or wandering off course. It required constant attention to fly accurately on instruments. For me, there was a fair amount of psychology involved. Apparently in World War I, the pilots were able to fly by "the seat of their pants," that is, they were able to judge the attitude of their aircraft by how they felt sitting in the aircraft seat. I found this not to be true when flying Mustangs. During my early days on the squadron, I was flying in heavy cloud at high altitude, feeling quite comfortable but not paying too much attention to my instruments, when I broke out of the cloud in a vicious diving turn. I was able to quickly pull out of the dive and straighten out, but I had not had any feeling at all that I was doing anything but flying straight and level. So much for the First World War-type of flying. There was a strong tendency to not believe one's instruments, several of which would have been indicating the problem. I found that I had to have explicit faith in my instruments, and not pay attention to unsupported feelings.

Flying in solid cloud for any prolonged period of time always gave me an almost claustrophobic feeling. I had to stare straight ahead at my flight instruments instead of continuously looking up and down and all around—a necessity when flying low level. Lack of having to fly IFR on most missions meant that we had to really concentrate when it was necessary for us to fly through solid cloud for any length of time. I had been flying in cloud for just a short while and already I was uncomfortable–when flying VFR, I didn't tire of flying.

Suddenly, the WAAF at Control called on the VHF to give me a course correction of a few degrees. I quickly made the correction, and continued my concentration on the flight instruments to compensate for the continual buffeting of the aircraft as it moved through the turbulent air currents in the cumulus nimbus clouds. The WAAF gave me three more course corrections over the next half hour or so, and I began to think that maybe she did know what she was doing.

Flying through the gloom of the cloud, I wondered how many other aircraft, enemy and allied, were in the cloud with me. If they were there, I could do nothing to avoid a collision. In peace time, all flights are regulated and under regional direction so that collisions can be avoided. In war time, there was no control over enemy flights, and even allied flight plans were intentionally kept secret. Our squadron had had one Mustang return from a flight through cloud with its coupe top VHF antenna broken off. The antenna extended just eighteen inches above the top of the coupe top—so you can imagine how close an encounter with something this represented.

By this time, I was bothered by two nagging questions. Had I overflown my base, and in danger of hitting the very high mountains in nearby Wales to the west? My fuel was very low, and would I soon have to force land or bail out when the engine quit? My thinking was interrupted by Control calling to instruct me to commence letting down to 2,000 feet. This was good news, but after flying at the lower altitude and still not able to see anything of the ground, I began to worry again that perhaps the cloud went right to ground level.

Unfortunately, there was no way to land an aircraft if you couldn't see the runway. I called Control and advised that I could see nothing. The WAAF advised me to continue letting down and that I was approaching my base. I figured she was probably sipping her tea while I was letting down a few hundred feet above who knows what, in an aircraft traveling at 300 m.p.h. or more and no visibility. I reduced speed and lowered the wheels and flaps in case I had to use them. I gritted my teeth and continued letting down, but I was ready to pull up quickly to avoid the anticipated crash— I was really low now.

Suddenly, the WAAF came on the radio to advise me that I was one half mile from the end of the runway, and that I should be able to see the flare path now. I strained my eyes and could see something, but I couldn't make it out clearly. Then I saw the welcome flares, but I was over the end of the runway now, and much too high. I knew that the cloud was far too low to risk having to go around again, and once away from the runway, I would never find the flare path again. I cut the throttle and went into a violent side slip to get rid of my excess height. I called the WAAF at Control and advised that I would be landing immediately. I thanked her for a job well done and remarked on her fantastic accuracy. When she had called, I must have indeed been a half mile from the end of the runway as she had advised. She came back to say that I was very welcome, and, I suppose, went back to her tea. I resolved not to be so reticent about using this homing service in the future—they did know what they were doing.

By the time I had slipped off the excess height and leveled off to touch down, there was less than half the runway left. I had to use the brakes pretty hard to stop just short of the boundary markers, but was finally able to turn off onto the taxi strip. The engine coughed a couple of times, indicating that it was sucking up the last of the fuel, but kept running. I proceeded around to dispersal where the aircraft were parked and the ground crew were waiting for me. As they were helping me with the harness, they remarked about the atrocious weather and inquired if it was as bad over the continent. I thought about sharing the recent events of the past few hours, but most people just never really understand. I had a rule against postmortems anyway, so I mentioned the only thing that I knew they would be interested in—my indeterminate encounter with the Heinkel.

15. The Mobile Aspect of Tactical Command

The fundamental function of Tactical Command was to provide close air support to the ground and sea forces in the assault against enemy forces. In order to do this, we had to move close behind our invading forces, operate from front line landing strips quickly built for the purpose, and be able to carry on complete operations from our own resources as the war required. We expected to move across to Europe after the invasion of the continent was launched and a large enough bridgehead had been established.

During the winter months, we were based on large permanent R.A.F. stations. These stations comprised of beautiful brick buildings with central heating, large messes and stone fireplaces—more for atmosphere than heat—and officers' quarters with single-occupancy rooms. All officers were provided with batmen or batwomen who shined shoes, polished uniform brass buttons and provided other supportive services. I was never too concerned about this service. I considered it a carry-over from the British Army operating in India—it went with their pink gin and polo. Canadians, on the whole, were not really spit-and-polish-type officers. They were more interested in flying functions than looking flashy. Rather than stiff and correct, a good flying-type hat, for instance, would be one that was well-broken in. R.A.F. Odiham was our home station and most of our winter operations were made from there.

During the summer months, we were under canvas, operating from many sites—mostly in southern England, north, west or south of London. Under canvas meant that all facilities were under canvas. The officers' mess was a large tent, as was the sergeants' and the men's mess. Small bell tents, with two officers per tent, were the sleeping quarters. It was quite pleasant most of the time, but I must say, during early spring and late fall, especially in November when the fog was heavy or gales howled, it wasn't the best.

We would drive to one of the outdoor ablution facilities about once a week for a leisurely bath. There were six or eight bathrooms with wooden walls raised eighteen inches up from the concrete floor, stopping eighteen inches from the roof shelter to allow the breezes full access. There was no shortage of hot water from the two-inch diameter pipes, and you could relax to your heart's content in the bath full of hot water. However, when you pulled the plug and started to dry yourself, you tended to move very quickly, and anything but leisurely. The British referred to the atmosphere as brisk.

Early morning fog was normal at this time of year, so everyone walked around in two or three feet of fog until the sun was warm enough to dissipate it. Some days, the fog would extend up to five hundred feet or so, and it would take quite a few hours to clear. This was quite frustrating, particularly if you had been up since 4:30 a.m. We had to keep our parachutes in our tent sleeping quarters. We had steel boxes to store them in, but the moist atmosphere penetrated everywhere. I did not expect to have to use my parachute, but if I ever did, I didn't want it to be too water-soaked to open. It was just another thing to be concerned about. To ease the situation, I made a practice of taking my parachute to the parachute tent more frequently than usual for drying out and repacking.

Following a very intensive period of operations during the autumn of 1943, when we concentrated on knocking out the V1 launching sites along the European coast, we were at the same time on standby to support a seagoing task force sent over to test the enemy defences along the Atlantic Wall.

The task force was made up of a few hundred ships, both naval and transport. From Southampton, they were to sail across the English Channel close to the French coast, and then, turn around without landing, and sail back to England. This was supposed to make the Germans think that it was the long awaited invasion. It was hoped that they would react and give their defence tactics away.

Actually, except for a lot of effort on our part having to chase their reconnaissance aircraft back across the channel several times per hour, little or nothing happened. The enemy didn't stay long enough over England for us to intercept them. Apart from trying to see just what was happening, the Germans ignored the task force, except when it ventured within gun range of the coast. While the task force was at sea, we stood by at Tangmere—two hours on and four hours off duty, around the clock—in an effort to control enemy activities. When the task force returned to port and our High Command was finally convinced that the Germans were not about to react, we stood down and were sent to R.A.F. Turnhouse, Edinburgh, Scotland, for Christmas rest.

Normally it was adequate for us to get airborne within three minutes after being scrambled, to intercept an incoming flight of enemy aircraft. This time we were expected to reach 30,000 feet within five minutes of being alerted. This meant that there would be no time for taxiing or engine warm-up. We had to sit at the end of the runway, and warm up the engine as required to enable immediate take-off anytime during the two-hour duty period. Having to sit in the aircraft, completely strapped in and ready to take off in the heat of the afternoon, wearing battle dress, Mae West life jacket and a parachute, was really something. The temperature reached 90° Fahrenheit that year, which was most unusual for England.

Some of our aircraft had been de-rated to 4,000 feet—that is, the engine developed maximum horsepower at this lower level. This was fine since most of the time we operated at zero feet, but in this case, it meant that our rate of climb dropped too drastically at the higher altitudes, giving the enemy time to escape.

Turnhouse was a very small aerodrome with extremely short runways. We had to keep the foot brake full on at the end of the runway, run the engine until the tail lifted, and then release the brakes to get airborne. Since we were not operational, and flying only to keep our hand in, we did not worry too much. Shortly after New Year's Day, we flew back to Odiham and were back on operations.

We frequently moved from airfield to airfield. Each time, we had to move everything—lock, stock and barrel. The move was usually done overnight so that we would be ready for full operations next morning. It wasn't a problem for the pilots. They simply flew their aeroplanes to the new aerodrome and carried on as usual. For the ground crew it was a different story. They had to pack everything in trucks and travel a few hundred miles, which took all night by road and only a few minutes by air.

When they finally arrived at the new site, they had to unpack and set up for operations, ready for when the pilots arose in the morning. There was no doubt that the pilots had the tougher job of the two.

16. The Survival Course

This course was given to our operational squadron to help us survive if we were shot down into enemy-occupied territory. The procedure was for us to attend a morning lecture given by various air force, army and naval officers who had recent information and/or personal experiences on the subject. In the afternoon, we would be dropped off in teams of two officers, at intervals along the highway, without our hats and instructed to try to get back to the Reading Police Station before dark without being caught by any of the police or military forces who had been alerted to watch for us.

As usual, I don't remember the name of the fellow I was with. Even though we considered the exercise a little silly, we decided to have a go at getting back to Reading. After walking a few miles, we were passing an R.A.F. airfield, and figured that if we could borrow a small plane, we would bypass all the police and troops looking for us, land at Reading Aerodrome and whip over to the police station.

We walked up to the gatehouse and even without our hats, were given a really sharp salute and allowed to pass. No one stopped us as we inspected the aircraft. Unfortunately, there were no Tiger Moths that we were looking for—only Wellington bombers and Beau fighter Night Fighters. We were not checked out on either of these aircraft, so we decided against stealing one, besides, we were not that desperate. We gave up and left the airfield, once again receiving a smart salute. Enlisted men were not supposed to salute an officer if he was not wearing his hat.

We found security extremely lax and I think we could have stolen any of the aircraft had we been more familiar with them. The ground crew would have helped us without questioning our authority. That was really scary.

We walked farther along the highway until we came to a small village. Since we hadn't had lunch, we dropped in to the local pub and had a sandwich. No one seemed to notice that we were officers without hats. They were all quite friendly as usual. We were many miles from Reading. It was getting late in the afternoon now, and as we didn't want to walk all the way, we left the pub and looked for a vehicle that we could borrow.

Although this was June 1943, and Britain had been at war for over four years now, the British people were fantastically open and trusting. We found a small car parked on the main street with all doors unlocked and the keys in the ignition. Unbelievable! We jumped in and took off down the highway toward Reading. Upon examination of the vehicle papers, we discovered that the car was owned by an officer of the Home Guard. He had left a beautiful joint—roast of beef—in the back seat that he was, I suppose, taking home for dinner. We couldn't do anything about the joint, but hoped that it would not spoil in the heat—it was obviously a very valuable item. I had never seen one in all the time I had been in England. Perhaps this would be a good lesson to this chap who was supposed to be guarding the homeland, not to live so carelessly—there was a war on.

We proceeded on towards Reading and noticed that there seemed to be more and more police and military vehicles on the road. We tried to look as nonchalant as possible as we drove along, but we certainly were being scrutinized by, it seemed, practically everyone. All of a sudden, an army motorcycle dispatch rider pulled alongside and looked at us very intently. I was driving, so I smiled at him, waved, and kept going. He speeded up and passed us. We figured that he must have been satisfied and we would be in Reading momentarily. A few miles further on, we came around a bend in the road and saw him manning a road-block with another motorcycle rider and a car. It crossed my mind to drive around, through the ditch, but I quickly dismissed it and came to a stop. It was bad enough that the Home Guard chap had almost lost his joint. I did not want to wreck his car too. The army dispatch rider was a Canadian and was smiling broadly when he greeted us. I don't remember who won that survival course back to Reading, but we certainly didn't. I can only hope that the fellow got his car and joint back safely.

When I was eventually shot down and had to survive, I did not, as I remember, use anything of what I learned on this practice run. The real thing demanded completely different decisions.

17. Suspicion of Sabotage

Returning to base after a short leave, I was informed that three Mustangs had crash-landed following engine failure on take-off, and sabotage was suspected. There was a real flap on. The R.A.F. Regiment responsible for airfield defence and security had been beefed up and there were armed troops everywhere. The gatehouse at the base entrance was manned by a very officious looking service police officer, instead of the usual sergeant, who demanded complete identification of everyone entering.

With the aircraft dispersed all around the boundaries of the two-mile-wide airfield, it was very difficult to provide twenty-four-hour surveillance, but it was being attempted from now on until the culprits were caught.

In the meantime, we had to live with the threat of engine failure on take-off, but more important to me, was the danger of the engine quitting over enemy territory. We certainly could not stop our operational flying. That is exactly what the enemy wanted to happen. Over the next ten days, one more aircraft crash-landed. The procedure when engine failure occurred at 500 feet or lower, was to keep the nose of the aircraft down, so as not to stall, and land straight ahead, avoiding, if possible, any obvious obstructions such as buildings and trees.

Turning back to land on the airfield, so as not to damage the aircraft was a definite No! No! With no engine, the turn would reduce airspeed to below the stall speed, and the aircraft would crash to the ground due to gravity, and the pilot would probably not survive. A normal, well-executed crash-landing in a Mustang, with wheels up, would damage the propeller blade ends, the under fuselage-mounted radiator, and not much else, plus the pilot could usually walk away on his own power.

A few days later, I was taking off and my engine suddenly stopped, but almost immediately started again. My right hand grabbed the fuel wobble pump handle on the side of the cockpit, and I pumped furiously. I don't know if the pump was helping, but the engine was still going, so I kept it up as I turned back to the airfield, but prepared to push the nose down and land straight ahead if the engine stopped again. As long as it kept running, I was going to try to get around the circuit and land into wind on the runway again. Keeping out from the line of aircraft hangers and the barracks, in case of engine problems requiring me to put down, I "wobble-pumped" my way along the downwind leg of the landing circuit, the cross-wind, and finally the approach, to safely touch down on the runway without the engine showing any sign of quitting. The intermittent nature of the problem was what was making it so difficult to solve. Engineering stripped down the engine, and examined each piece in detail, but found nothing.

About a week later, another Mustang engine failed, not on take-off, but on the approach to land. The pilot landed dead stick, without engine, on the runway without any trouble, and stopped in the middle of the runway. The aeroplane was towed directly to the hanger for dismantling. This time they found the problem—quantities of water in the petrol in just about all of the fuel lines. An investigation was launched immediately.

Four-wheel petrol bowsers, towed by tractors, were used on the airfield to refuel the aircraft. They were out in the rain most of the time, servicing the widely-dispersed aircraft. It was finally discovered that the gasket on one of the filler hatches on one of the petrol bowsers was defective, allowing the rain water to leak in and mix with the petrol.

Sabotage not being involved, tight security was relaxed and the airfield returned to normal. We all felt relieved that now, although we would still have our normal operational concerns to contend with, engine failure due to water in our fuel, would not be one of them.

18. D-Day : The Invasion of Europe: *Operation Overlord*

A special squadron duty, was a one-day function performed on D-Day, June 6, 1944—the day the Allied Forces landed on the Normandy beaches in an all out attempt to drive the enemy out of the occupied countries to final defeat. Our operating base for the invasion was Tangmere, a fighter base on the channel in southern England. We were ordered there from our home base of Odiham on the afternoon of June 4th. The invasion was scheduled for dawn, June 5th, when the phase of the moon would cause the lowest tides for the period, so that our landing craft could unload the troops on the beach before they hit the enemy's steel underwater obstructions.

As I circled the field to land, I noticed the lashing rain and huge waves in the channel and wondered just how the small landing craft was going to make it onto the beaches without capsizing. The Supreme Commander, General Eisenhower, finally had to cancel all plans for June 5th because of the stormy weather. Marginal improvement was expected in twenty-four hours, so everything was re-scheduled for June 6th. This presented a real security problem since hundreds of thousands of army, navy and air force personnel had been fully briefed on the invasion plans before the postponement. Everyone was confined to their ship, camp, or base for the twenty-four hours, and though it was boring and very restrictive, no one wanted the enemy to find out that we were coming.

Our squadron's function was to direct the naval guns of the hundreds of battleships, cruisers, and destroyers, which would be steaming at high speed back and forth, a few miles off the Normandy invasion beaches, onto pre-selected enemy targets on shore. In April, 1944, the squadron had been sent to Llanbedrog, Wales, to learn how to quickly and accurately direct shells onto floating targets in the Irish Sea, using two heavy cruisers. We would control the ship's guns by giving them the map references of the target and first asking for a single shot. We would organize our flying so that we could observe the target close up just when we judged the shell would arrive. If the shot was short of the target by say 400 yards, and to the left by 600 yards, we would call for a correction of up 400 and right 600. The gunners would fire a second single round and if it wasn't on target, we would give a correction again. The number of yards was of course an estimate and accuracy had to be learned. The corrections invariably resulted in the shots bracketing the target at first. In time, though, we were able to judge the distances better so that we brought the shots quickly to target center. The final order to the gunners would be for a volley—all guns firing at the registered direction and range. We would do this in Normandy, but while training, we did not want to destroy the target, so we did not call for the volley.

Later in the afternoon of June 5, when it·was confirmed that the invasion was on for June 6, all of the air crew of R.A.F. Tactical Command were assembled out in the middle of the aerodrome for security reasons, and also because there were too many to accommodate anywhere else. The sun had come out, and we were sitting on the grass between the intersecting runways. Our chief, Air Vice-Marshall Leigh-Mallory wanted to talk to us before we went into action the next morning. He advised that in the past, very large confrontations with the enemy had resulted in far too many "friendly-fire" casualties—allied forces firing on their own people, mistaking them for the enemy. To keep these casualties to a minimum, and to make our aircraft stand out from the enemy, three wide, white paint stripes were to be applied to the top and bottom of the wings on all Allied aircraft. In this way, our forces would not have to rely on I.F.F. identification only, but could simply refrain from firing at white-striped aircraft, and empty their guns at aircraft not so identified, making for far less chance of an error. To prevent the enemy copying this invasion stripe identification, the ground crews would be doing the painting at the last possible minute. The problem was that the paint could not possibly dry in the cool wet night air. At 4:30 a.m. the next morning, as I jumped up on the wing of my aircraft to climb into the cockpit and get airborne, my heel skidded on the wet paint, and I just about fell into the slowly revolving propeller.

The Marshall really cheered us up by telling us that it was expected that Tactical Command would experience 50% casualties. I realized that that included me, but in my usual optimistic thinking, felt that it certainly was unfortunate for the persons sitting each side of me. The reason that pilots and air crew always appeared to rather callously handle news of the death of one of their own, was that they realized that although it was now over for their friend, they themselves had to face a possible similar fate tomorrow, the next day or the next, or the next, and no one felt all that confident.

We were over the invasion beaches at dawn on June 6th. We had been given a number of enemy targets to engage using the ships' naval guns. We did not know which naval ship would respond, but simply used code names to order aiming shots and then corrections, as required, to guide the shots onto the targets one at a time. When the shots hit dead center, we would order full volleys until we were satisfied that the target was destroyed. The Germans had protected some of their big guns with four to six feet of concrete. If we noticed any activity on a target we thought had been destroyed, we would order another volley on this target, and although the naval ship had obviously been steaming back and forth off the beaches in the meantime, the shells arrived once again dead center of the target. The gunners were very good. Just after dawn, the small tank and personnel landing craft headed for the beaches along the whole length of Normandy and the invasion was on. I will never forget the sight of the fantastic turmoil going on below us.

The troops landing on the beaches beneath me were obviously having their troubles, but all I could do was to do my job well to knock out the enemy coastal guns which were firing on the beach. I tried to keep my ship's guns firing right up to the last minute—it was extremely difficult to silence the enemy guns. Although the low tide made the wide expanse of sandy beach visible, it was hard to see what was happening because of all the smoke and the many explosions. Many of the landing craft had been hit, and were burning on the beach, and out in the water. I was able to finally get a shell on to the center of my last target, and because I assumed that our forces must be well up on the beaches by now, I gave the naval cruiser firing, an order to fire one last volley—all guns firing, and then to cease firing and stand down to ensure that I was not firing on our troops.

I think we were pretty successful at knocking out the big enemy guns, but small arms and machine guns still remained, and caused tremendous casualties, as troops swarmed up the beaches.

I did not know it when I flew over that morning, but the first troops to hit the beach at Juno, the Canadian beach, were the Queen's Own Rifles, the division that I spent thirty days in training with back in 1940. They sustained many casualties, so it is just as well that I didn't stay with them, as I couldn't really have done much with just a rifle and a bayonet. At least flying over them, I was able to help eliminate the big guns.

In actual fact, except for the possibility that I could be hit by the naval shells I was guiding, or perhaps colliding with one of the hundreds of our own aircraft, also screaming back and forth over the beaches trying to accomplish their missions, I found my flying on D-Day, if anything, easier than my normal missions. There was no difficult navigation involved. I just followed the thousands of ships in the channel to the target. There was no long range problem where you could run short of fuel, and there were, apparently, no enemy fighters to worry about.

Although I am sure that the saturation bombing and even the naval shelling did not completely destroy all the enemy guns trained on the beaches, our efforts did, I believe, keep their heads down, so that our troops could have time to land on the beaches, unload their equipment, and overrun the enemy positions. I signaled my No. 2 that we would return to base. As we flew low over a cruiser, I was astounded to see them firing at us. The good old navy! They didn't know a Mustang from a Focke-Wulf 190! Luckily, they did not hit us.

Of course, we were never to fly over a capital ship, but with wall-to-wall battleships in the channel, it was just about impossible to go around, besides we were low on fuel. We made two more missions to the beaches before the day was over. Except for a few Junker 88 light bombers, I saw no enemy aircraft over the beaches during my sorties on D-Day. Since the Germans had made capturing a port too costly, we were forced to invade via the empty Normandy beaches. Our forces needed huge amounts of fuel to move the tanks, ships and transports. To provide for this, the Allies floated a monstrous refueling dock all the way over to Cherbourg, connected to a port in England by a fuel line lying on the bottom of the channel, to supply their requirements. Flying over the next day, I was amazed at the size of it as it was being towed over.

19. Consolidating the Normandy Beachhead

Our function, now that the beachhead was established, was to provide Headquarters with everything and anything that the enemy was doing in reaction to the beachhead. It was going to take time to build up our strength there, and for the first few days it would be touch and go. The Germans had two complete armies in the Calais area. Hitler expected the Allies to invade across the shortest route to the continent—Dover to Calais. The Allies gave him every opportunity to think this by stationing General George Patton and his 3rd Army at Dover until sometime in July, when they embarked for the beachhead. They were replaced by dummy masses of equipment—wooden and cardboard tanks, guns, and thousands of empty tents. At zero feet, they were obviously dummies, but at the 30,000-foot position of the enemy reconnaissance planes, it looked as if General Patton's army was still there. Spitfire patrols over Dover made sure that the enemy was never allowed a closer look. The British were very good at this kind of deception. It effectively kept Hitler's most powerful armies out of the fighting, enabling us to win with much lower casualties on both sides.

For the next few days, we had to fly endless missions all across France to find out if anything was being moved to join the invasion battle. The usual method of moving troops through France was via Paris on the railway system. With the use of our Rhubarbs, we pretty well stopped this. We monitored the River Seine everyday to see if they were coming across country and building bridges. All of our reports were negative—nothing was moving. Each time I returned from a reconnaissance, I would be met by a bevy of briefing officers, all anxious to hear where the enemy was coming from, and how. Everyone expected that the German forces opposing us in Normandy would be reinforced—why wasn't it happening? I assured them that I had just checked Calais, and not only were the forces there not on the move, but there were indications that they were digging in deeper. Hitler obviously considered Normandy a diversion and the real assault was about to be launched from Dover, across to Calais where he would be ready.

Although the beachhead was very limited in depth, our engineers had managed to construct a small landing strip. It was made of very heavy gauge steel mesh. The Germans used Junkers 88s to bomb the beachhead many times each day. A hit on the landing strip would cause a big hole in the steel mesh and the earth beneath, but could be patched very successfully by simply fastening a piece of new mesh over the hole. The landing surface was wavy but smooth enough to safely land very soon after a bombing.

So as not to be encumbered with long range fuel tanks which had to be jettisoned when attacked, we were ordered to refuel at the beachhead landing strip before crossing the channel to our base in England. From the air, the strip looked about the size of a postage stamp, with the enemy artillery lines about a hundred yards away. Coming in low and fast, I would whip the wheels and flaps down and land as quickly as I could, so they would not have time to shoot. It was no time for by-the-book landings. I made some very unorthodox touchdowns on the strip. After a two-hour mission, I was glad to relax while my aircraft was refueled and armed. My rest didn't last long though. The beachhead ground crew consisted of twenty men, instead of the usual two or three back at the base. In a few minutes, they were shouting for me to get airborne again, to make way for incoming aircraft. The fewer planes on the strip, the better, in case the enemy decided to bomb again.

20. Hitler's Secret Weapons

On the evening of June 13th, 1944, an aircraft flew very low over the base. We were relaxing in the officers' mess when it flew over, and we all remarked how strange it sounded. There was a thunderous explosion a few seconds later, so we knew that it hadn't made it over Red Hill which was just north of the base. We walked up to the crash site on the side of the hill. All we found was a very large crater and no sign of an aircraft. Next morning, the radio and the newspapers reported that it was a crashed Junkers 88, but we realized that it was probably the first flight of Hitler's secret weapon, the VI Pilotless Aircraft. The VI carried a ton of explosives, was jet-engine driven, held to a set course by a simple automatic pilot and with its range determined by the amount of fuel put into the tank. With a little more fuel, we estimated that it would have cleared the hill and gone on to its intended target—London.

From the autumn of 1943 through to the end of May, 1944, we had been monitoring Hitler's efforts to build launching sites for these weapons along the European coast. Each site consisted of a huge fixed launching ramp, probably aimed at London, and a hockey stick-shaped storage shed. We would go in fast at zero feet and photograph the site, watching the hundreds of construction workers scurry away. Our pictures were used by several Boston light bomber squadrons who were kept busy all winter trying to destroy hundreds of these sites along the French and Belgium coastal areas. Two weeks, or so, after a site was bombed, we would return to find that the site had been rebuilt, and it would be bombed again.

The Germans used fantastic amounts of manpower—probably prisoners—to rebuild these sites as fast as we destroyed them. I am not sure that we won this battle, because on June 13, 1944, they launched the first VI Buzz Bomb. The barrage was to continue at about twenty-minute intervals around the clock, until the sites were overrun by our troops. Many of these missiles were shot down by the British coastal artillery batteries, many by our fast flying Tempests. Unfortunately, the majority got through to further devastate London's civilian population. When I got back from France in September, the V1s were still coming over at about the same intervals. The Air Commodore, who was debriefing me at Air Ministry in London, stopped talking when a V1 came over and the missile's engine stopped, meaning that it was diving straight down. After the explosion proved that it had not hit the Air Ministry, but a building about a block away, he carried on talking, as if nothing had happened. The V1 had that effect on everyone.

We had also been active in photographing Hitler's other secret weapon, the V2, which was an actual rocket fueled by a solid propellant designed to be fired a few miles into space on a ballistic trajectory, terminating, once again, in the battered city of London. The V2 rocket sites were based much farther back from the coast. As for the V1—the only way to stop them was for our troops to overrun the launching sites.

21. My Final Mission

On Sunday, June 18th, 1944, I was about to embark on my third and final mission for the day. As it turned out, it was final in more ways than one. The mission was not expected to be a difficult one. It was simply to verify the week's observations—that there was no troop movement through the train junction south of Paris. I was not planning to use my camera, as it would be too dark by the time I would be in the area.

The mission was to be visual only. I was instructed to fly at very high speed, very low, over the target, and observe everything in the scene displayed before me. I had a reporting pad strapped to my knee, and a pencil in my hand. Even though I was busy flying and trying not to hit anything, including the ground, my eyes, somehow, saw everything. The information was transmitted to my brain, and somehow, when I climbed away from the target, a fantastic amount of data, such as the number of train cars in the yard, their contents—troops, tanks, guns, and ammunition—was written on the knee pad. It is a matter of training and effort, of course. The first time I tried this, I managed to record only one squiggly line. My brain had been busy doing other things. Eventually, I became very good and didn't question what was recorded.

On this particular day, my No. 2, Flight Lieutenant Vernon Lewis and I set out on our mission about 9:30 p.m.. Crossing the French coast, we encountered some flak, but weren't hit. Several miles inland from the coast, my No. 2 called to advise that he had become separated from me. I don't believe that we had flown through cloud, but it was now very late in the day, and there was a low ceiling of heavy black cloud making visibility difficult. Line abreast battle formation was only possible when pilots could see each other. I, therefore, called my No. 2 and instructed him to return to base, but I was loath to abort the mission. I reasoned that if my No. 2 couldn't see me, the enemy pilots couldn't see me either.

I called my No. 2 and gave him the magnetic course to steer for home while I continued on to the target alone.

The target—the rail junction at Versailles—was the site of Germany's surrender to the Allies, in a specially outfitted railroad car, at the end of the First World War in 1918. It was, also, the same location where Hitler accepted France's surrender in 1940.

Flight Lieutenant Vernon Lewis was a very good pilot, but since most of his concentration had been directed to formatting on me, I suspected that he might have become disoriented upon separation. I called him a few more times to help him get home. I fully expected to be on my way home soon, too. As I approached the train junction, I increased speed and dived down to observe the activity below.

The flak came up to meet me and appeared to be heavier than usual. Maybe they were trying to hide something. As I passed over the multiple train tracks and started to climb away, I received a hit at the front of the aircraft. The engine stopped immediately with a violent shudder, and I could hardly see for the smoke. I used my momentum to gain as much height as possible to give my parachute time to open. It was not a time to wonder what I was going to do. It was a matter of thinking when there's no time to think. I had to get the most height I could, but if I tried for too much height, I would get below flying speed and stall back to earth. Getting out of a stalled Mustang would not be successful.

On the way up, I got rid of the coupe top by selecting "open," and punching up as hard as I could. The coupe top went straight up and back. I set the elevator trim control to nose heavy, so that when I let go of the stick, the tail would rise quickly and I would not be impaled on the tailplane when I bailed out. I went quickly over the side and was quite relieved to see the underside of the tailplane flash by. Because I was so low to the ground, I pulled the rip-cord as soon as I passed the tailplane. I was still travelling forward at a fair speed, and when the parachute opened, the resulting jolt just about stopped my breathing. However, the fact that it had opened at all was a relief. I floated for a few seconds feeling really good—everything was quiet and peaceful—the roar of the engine and the impact of the shell resulted in me being stone deaf for a day or so.

The floating feeling was short-lived. I saw the tops of the trees go by and then I hit the ground and bounced a good four feet. A pilot's parachute is just large enough to prevent him from being killed, not for a comfortable landing—I hit the ground, hard. I had come down in a field a mile or so from the perimeter of the Marshalling Yards. I gathered up my parachute and hid it in the trees so that it wouldn't be found readily. I decided to get out of the area as fast as possible. I headed roughly west, away from where my aircraft crashed and I never saw it again.

When a pilot bails out of his aircraft and his parachute opens and saves his life, he becomes a member of the "Caterpillar Club." If the parachute does not open and he is killed, the Irvine Company's warranty allows him to visit the factory and receive a full refund of the purchase price. You can't beat that, eh!

22. On My Own

I walked all the rest of the night in spite of a sore ankle I sprained on landing. I kept away from all towns, villages and highways to avoid being spotted by roving patrols. At dawn, I lay down and slept in the trees, well back from the highway. Later on in the day, I picked up the telephone and called room service to order bacon and eggs with all the trimmings for breakfast—didn't I wish!

Before leaving on an operational mission, a pilot is given an emergency kit, containing several small squares of chocolate, a tube of condensed milk paste, a pouch with purifying tablets to make the local water safe to drink, a few cigarettes and a wad of money in the currency of the country to be flown over. For this particular mission, I had 4,000 French francs. Also in the kit was a handkerchief-sized map of France made of pure silk and a walking-style compass. All of this was packaged in a pocket-sized plastic container to fit the breast pocket of my battle dress to ensure it would be handy after bailing out. The R.A.F. flying boots were made in two parts; the shoe part, and the top part that encased the calf. The two parts were sewn together and could be separated by cutting the thread. The top part could be removed to leave a reasonable-looking pair of oxfords, which could pass for civilian shoes.

Since I had not heard from room service, I decided to get breakfast myself. I had one chocolate square and a small squirt of milk paste. There was a small stream nearby, so I was able to drink all the water I wished. I used a purifying tablet in the pouch and the water tasted fine. I felt that I had better keep moving. I passed a small herd of cattle a short distance upstream from where I'd obtained the drinking water—I hoped that the purifying tablets had been effective. Walking parallel to the highway, but in the bushes so that I could see but not be seen, I was startled to observe that the people walking along the side of the highway all wore wooden clogs, which made their steps sound more like horses trotting than people walking. For a moment, I thought that my navigational skills had failed me and that I had actually come down in Holland instead of France. I quickly realized that this was impossible—my navigation had never been that bad! By walking all night, I had moved away from urban Paris into the rural farming area where, I suppose, farm people wore clogs because of the mud, just as they did in Holland.

By late afternoon, I figured that I was far enough away from the crash area to relax and plan what I was going to do next. While at the squadron base, I had attended many briefings about what we should do if shot down over enemy occupied territory. I hadn't paid much attention, because I didn't plan for it to happen to me.

Every briefing advised giving oneself up to the enemy and volunteering name, rank and number, only. Although I usually followed most of the tactical flying advice without question, I decided that giving myself up to a desperate, ruthless enemy was not going to be my decision. I decided to head for the coast, and try to get on board one of the small fishing boats that I had noticed many times when I had crossed the channel. I used to wave to the fisherman, and usually, they would wave back. I imagined that this gave them hope for the future.

We were also advised to stay in uniform or we would run the risk of being shot as a spy. I knew that I couldn't possibly evade capture unless I got rid of my uniform. Even after I had removed my wings and rank markings, I stood out from the sea of drab clothes worn by the French civilians that I had observed. I selected a poorly-equipped farm—no wires running to the house and buildings, therefore no telephone, so they couldn't call the police—and approached the farmer to buy civilian clothes.

Although I had taken French at school and remembered most of the commonly used words, I did not think my conversational French was going to fool anyone. I, therefore, did everything with hand signals, pointing to the farmer's suit and hat. Although, I'd removed all air force markings from my battle dress, I could see in his eyes, that he knew who and what I represented. I did not feel at all secure. The farmer readily agreed to my request, and gave me a worn suit and a beret for a few hundred francs. The suit more or less fit me and the beret really made me look French!

After changing into the suit, I removed my wrist watch, my identification bracelet, and my mother's gold wedding ring that my father had given to me before I went overseas. These were very valuable to me, so I wrapped them in a handkerchief and kept them in my pants pocket the whole time that I was in France. It was one of the few stupid things I did, I realize now. What would I have done if I had been arrested and searched? The appearance of being just another Frenchman would have been instantly destroyed. I suppose that I was just too much of a Scotsman to throw them away, which, obviously, I should have done.

I continued walking west, and a half mile further on, I threw my uniform down an unused well. I wanted to get out of the area quickly, just in case the helpful farmer was a collaborator, and wanted to stay in good with the enemy. He might have been perfectly alright, as most of the poor farmers were—it was the middle class that you had to watch. However, I felt that I could not take a chance.

Along the way, I tried to supplement my meals of one chocolate square and a squirt of milk paste with what I could find, but nothing growing in the fields was edible—at least not to me. It all appeared to be cattle feed. The turnips and cabbages were really rough. I finally came upon a small garden with a few rows of carrots. They were very good and tender. I took all of them. The poor farmer must have wondered what happened. Each meal could now be topped off with a juicy carrot. What more could one want?

I don't remember too much about this period of the journey, except that as I got closer and closer to the coast, security got tighter and tighter. There were check points on every road leading to the coast. Since I had no identity papers, I couldn't hope to get past them. I had been on my own for eight days and I was getting nowhere. I finally realized that I was going to have to get help to get out of the country.

23. Attempting to Reach the French Resistance Movement

I knew about the existence of the French Resistance Movement, the *maquis,* but I did not know how to contact them, who to trust, and who was in league with the enemy. By now, my beard had grown and, once again, I stood out from the crowd, as most Frenchmen were clean shaven. I decided to approach the children at the local school. If they appeared hostile I could quickly get away, and they couldn't stop me. I would be on the run once more, but I had confidence that I could evade capture in the bush.

At the next village, I carefully checked the presence of the enemy and except for a few Germans at one end of the village, the school, which was at the other end, seemed to be clear. I walked into the school yard and in French—more or less—asked a small group of children if they would please get their teacher for me. After eight days on the road, I was much bolder than I had been.

Thankfully, the children understood my halting French immediately. They disappeared into the school. Seconds later, their teacher came rushing out. She seemed very excited, and because I couldn't understand a word she said, she gave up, and pulled me bodily into the school. I eventually gathered that the Germans were closer than I thought. The woman was joined by a second teacher and together they got through to me, in French—no one spoke any English—that this was a German-occupied village, and that there were no Resistance people within thirty kilometres or so.

One of the teachers took me out the back door of the school, and down the street to a building where the women of the village did their washing, a community affair. I was concerned that the children, who had witnessed our talk at the school and were really excited, would be talking too much, but the teacher assured me that the children knew the dangers and nothing would happen. I had my first solid food in eight days, complete with a bowl—they didn't seem to use cups—of ersatz coffee laced with wine. I had mentioned that I had to shave, so the other teacher went home to get her husband's shaving gear. Unfortunately, it was a straight razor and not too sharp. My hand shook as I scraped my face clean again.

The teachers advised me that they knew of a Resistance group in a town called Rouillac, situated beside two small lakes, about thirty-five kilometres south of their village. I thanked everyone present—all the women in town must have been there by this time—and left immediately.

Using my compass, I headed south to Rouillac. At one point, I was about to cross the highway, when, for some reason, I hesitated in the bushes along the ditch. I don't know why I held back, but it was a good thing that I did. A squad of German troops rounded the corner, armed to the teeth and flanked by two non-combatants on bicycles. I stayed still and watched them march by. Now I knew why I hadn't seen many troops in town. Had I dashed across the highway, I might have escaped into the bush, but the soldiers, with their automatic rifles, would have had the edge, I'm afraid.

I don't remember just how long it took me to get to Rouillac, but by now, I was travelling night and day. The teachers had advised that, when I arrived in Rouillac, I should go to the church and speak to the priest. As usual, I made sure there were no Germans visible near or around the church, and then walked up to the priest at the door, and inquired about the Resistance group. I was getting more and more frustrated after eight days of getting nowhere, and probably showed my impatience when talking to the priest in my broken French. In any case, instead of answering me, he had a terrified look in his eyes, and stepped back into the church and closed the door. I immediately suspected that I'd walked into a trap. I hurried away as fast as I could without actually running, as this would really attract attention.

I decided to get out of this town as quickly as possible. I had only gone about one hundred yards, when a man caught up with me and started talking excitedly. He was speaking in French, and I could only understand a small part of it. In essence, he said that he was glad to meet me, and that I should get off the street and go with him. At this stage, I really didn't trust anyone, but I had just walked thirty-five kilometres to get the Resistance to help me, so I had to take a chance. I found out later that he didn't trust me either. A favourite trick of the Germans was to plant a Gestapo agent, pretending to be a bailed-out pilot and who could speak perfect English, in the Resistance groups, in order to betray and destroy them.

As a result of their doubts and fears, I was kept in a house in town for three days. Although they were pleasant and I was fed well, they really didn't commit themselves. I was continually interrogated by them—but not in an obvious way. They wanted to know what was playing at the Palladium in London, and such things, so that they would know, I suppose, if I had been in England recently as I claimed. The problem was that I did not give any of the correct answers. I had been flying night and day for the past three or four months with no time at all to visit London, or any other place. In spite of my failing to correctly answer just about everything they asked me, they finally appeared to believe that I was indeed a downed R.A.F. pilot, and not a danger to them.

That evening, I was visited by about a dozen people. We all shook hands and celebrated with a drink of what seemed to me to be pure gasoline. A few days later, I was advised that I would be going to Bordeaux and on, to escape through Spain.

As a result of the Spanish Civil War of 1936 to 1939, General Franco, with the more or less unofficial help of Germany's Hitler and Italy's Mussolini, defeated the loyalist troops and became dictator of Spain. Hitler used this conflict to train his pilots and test his war equipment for the battles to come. Even though Spain was definitely fascist and pro-Germany, they had to appear neutral. Escapees using the route out of France to Spain were usually thrown into jail. The Spanish jails were really miserable by our standards, but after a week or so, prisoners were released upon demand from the British Embassy. I was all for having a go.

I was advised that walking was the only mode of travel available to me. I already understood why I wouldn't be taking the train. I was guided by a member of the Resistance who would take me a few kilometres—fifteen to twenty—to the next point in the escape route, where he would hand me over to another member, who would accompany me over the next leg of the journey. Each guide knew only the identity of his contacts and no others. This was done to prevent the Gestapo from being able to extract anything but limited information from anyone they captured. Unfortunately, the Gestapo did arrest one or more of the guides a few days later, which meant that I could not go on, and I had to return to Rouillac.

With the escape through Spain aborted, I was guided to Finistère, Brittany, where I was placed with a farmer, Pierre Lacheur, and his mother. The Lacheur farm was about a mile away from the town of Morlaix, where there was a very active Gestapo Headquarters. I had to be hidden every night in case the Gestapo visited. My hiding place was above a cattle stable where I had a cot in a hollowed out space in the firewood. The firewood, which consisted of mainly small tree branches, was full of rats that made a real racket scurrying around. Before retiring each night, I would have to beat the firewood walls with a big stick to settle them down, so that I could get to sleep. Other than that, the rats kept to themselves and did not bother me. With a bunch of Gestapo thugs less than a mile away, I certainly was not going to lose any sleep over a few rats.

Access to the loft above the stable was through a trapdoor in the stable ceiling. I had to hoist myself up through the trapdoor, and as I did so, the cows would invariably squeeze together so that I couldn't make it. I would have to drop down again, and push them far enough apart so that I could get up before they had time to squeeze in again and stop me. I guess they were just too friendly. They were French longhorns and didn't look all that friendly. I tended them in the fields, just to keep busy. If I didn't keep a close eye on them, they would get over the hedge fence, or the young ones would bump me from behind. I had to be very careful not to shout at them in English.

Pierre's mother's house was a two-bedroom farmhouse. The upstairs was quite neat and tidy with varnished hardwood floors. Shoes, or in most cases, clogs had to be removed before going upstairs. The downstairs floor was earthen with an open fireplace where all the cooking had to be done. Madame Lacheur swept the earth floor every day.

Pierre, although only twenty-three years of age, was in charge of a Resistance district, comprised of four *maquis* groups of about two hundred men each. I spent about a week and a half with Pierre and his mother. They could speak only French, so out of necessity, my French got better and better. Pierre and I spent a great deal of time discussing communism versus democracy. Although the *maquis* had loads of communistic literature, I suppose printed in Russia and provided by the Russians for political reasons, I did not consider them Russian Communists, but French Nationalists. They were the only ones fighting the enemy for France. The majority of the French people had given up and were collaborating with the Germans.

I am not sure why I thought it was my duty to defend democracy. I suppose it was because Pierre appeared to really want to know. My discussions with Pierre covered the whole gambit of the finer points of communism and democracy. Russia was an ally of ours at this time, so I tried not to criticize too much. I think Pierre understood. My French was pretty good now, although I did use quick ways of getting my point across, and it probably wasn't always good French. About halfway through my stay with Pierre and his mother, I stopped translating everything they said to me into English, and could answer directly in French. I could almost dispense with my usual opening statement of, *"Vous parlez trop vite,"* (you speak too quickly), but not quite—the French people speak very quickly at the best of times.

Pierre Lacheur's ambition was to enter politics after the war. However, at the close of the war, the *maquis* were disarmed, and even though they were the only ones in France that had fought for their country, they were branded as Communists, particularly by the Americans, who had a tremendous fear of "Commies" of any kind. The Americans preferred fascists, even ex-German officers, for some reason, ignoring the fact that they were probably war criminals. The thousands of French officials, who had disgracefully collaborated with the enemy against their own people, all during the war, did not want the ex-Resistance Fighters in power, as they knew they would be punished for their treason. They didn't even want known war criminals brought to trial, as this would undoubtedly expose their own conduct during the war. Thus, everything was kept quiet. The Resistance was frozen out of politics, and General De Gaulle, with the help of the very officials that sided with the Germans during the war years, ruled France.

They claim that as many as 10,000 French collaborators were executed, or at least brought to justice, at the end of the war. You can be sure that they were not the real war criminals—only those that were not powerful, or rich enough, to be able to bribe their way out of trouble.

As I remember, General De Gaulle spent the war in London, England, representing the Free French, whoever they were. They were apparently not the French Resistance, which fought the Germans inside France all during the war. When the Allies took Paris, General De Gaulle marched victoriously at the head of his troops down the Champs-Élysées, with no *maquis* to be seen.

Whenever I got to London, I would always buy copies of the four or five morning newspapers. *The Mirror* was similar to present-day tabloids, which concentrated on sensational news events, but the remainder were informative and very well written. I followed the progress of the war with great interest. The meetings of Churchill, Roosevelt, King, Stalin and other Allied leaders were reported, to the extent that they could be reported, without giving away plans to the enemy. The stories invariably recorded agreement between all the Allied leaders, except General De Gaulle, who always disagreed with everything. Since France was not in a position to help defeat the enemy—they had had their chance in 1940—the General was pretty well ignored.

I had been waiting for the re-establishment of the escape route to Spain, but from all reports, the Gestapo were getting more and more active. The Resistance in Bordeaux had been decimated and many on the escape line had been arrested and were expected to be shot. That was the Germans' answer to everything.

German SS troops and Gestapo from Morlaix stepped up their patrols of the area and visited Madame Lacheur during the week while I was out tending the cows. They didn't appear to be looking for anything in particular. I suppose they thought that no one would be hiding a downed pilot so close to their headquarters. They looked through the house and ignored the stable, but, obviously, there were going to be a lot more searches in the future. Anyone helping a person such as me, was shot immediately, if caught. I did not want anything to happen to the Lacheurs. They had risked their lives for me long enough. I felt that there was no time to lose, so I suggested to Pierre that he take me to one of the *maquis* camps. He agreed and we left immediately for one not too far away.

24. Joining the "Giles" Jedburgh Team at the Maquis Camp

The camp was a farm like the one I had just left. It was not as close to the main highway, and there were only a few farm animals. In the barn and the various outbuildings, were a hundred or so *maquis* members. I had to meet and shake hands with every one of them. They were either ex-French Army, Navy or Air Force people or very young boys who wanted to fight to free France from the Germans. The leader was an ex-French Submarine Captain who had walked away when France surrendered. Except for the young members, most had been fighting the Germans from the hills and the forests since the surrender in 1940.

Also at the camp was a three-man Jedburgh Team, with code name "Giles" from the Office of Strategic Service (O.S.S.), who had parachuted out of the U.S.A. A.F. Liberator on July 9, 1944 into Finistère, Brittany. Their mission was to raise and supply an army made up of the men from the local *maquis*. Arms, explosives, and equipment would be dropped to them, but they were not to engage in open warfare with the Germans, until they got the O.K. via the BBC. The signal, which would unleash them against the Germans, was *"Le chapeau de Napoleon est-il toujours a Perros-Guirec?"*

I rushed up to the farmhouse to meet these people, feeling that, finally, we would get something done. The leader of the team was an American, Major Knox, who had served with the loyalists in the Franco-Spanish War and who spoke French beautifully. He was assisted by a Frenchman, Captain Labelle, who had been born in the area and knew it like a book, and an Englishman, Sergeant Tack, who was their wireless operator (W.T.).

Major Knox advised that the Allies were using four-engine aircraft—Lancaster, Halifax and Sterling bombers—to parachute in large canisters containing badly needed arms, such as Bazookas,

Bren machine guns, Sten machine guns, ammunition, plastic explosives, army boots and other equipment. His immediate requirement was to select suitable drop sites or zones to be used, preferably remote and on high ground, and transmit their location—map coordinates—to London for future drops.

Although the *maquis* groups had the will to fight, they were ill-equipped, untrained, and without discipline. Their little French pistols, smaller than .22 inch, were useless against the German arms. They did, however, have a few good cooks, and even a camp barber.

There were always two or three women, either wives or daughters of the *maquis* men, staying at each camp. They were used as couriers to transmit messages from one camp to the other, and to gather information. They rode bicycles and could get past any of the road blocks. The Germans never seemed to bother them, whereas a male courier would be arrested every time. However, when the *maquis* really began to harass them, the Germans sent 20,000 troops to destroy the Resistance, and many of these women were killed without mercy.

During the day at the camp, the men were given instructions regarding the care and use of the many weapons dropped to them. At night, a squad of men would be out patrolling an area to check on German activity, but were forbidden to interfere. The Major and I went along on these patrols to keep abreast of what was going on. We were marching along, supposedly quietly, past a village which we knew contained a German post, and all of a sudden, one of the men's guns fired all on its own. One night, one of the men shot himself in the knee. Believe it or not, he continued the march and was patched up when he got back to camp, apparently not badly injured. Obviously their guns wouldn't stop very much. I was more afraid of the *maquis* than the enemy on these patrols. It was a good thing that the German sentries were sound sleepers.

Sergeant Tack was equipped to pick up the signals from the BBC and had a transmitter to send the W.T. signal. Both were powered by a hand-driven generator. I would turn the generator handle while the Sergeant sent the messages. The messages were mostly map references to drop sites suitable for the bombers to drop the needed weapons and ammunition, and were directed to the O.S.S. division of the War Office in London. The Sergeant sent all messages in code taken directly from a code book, which could only be decoded from a similar book in the War Office. No amount of normal code-breaking skills could hope to break the code, and the code books were changed frequently. The system used the BBC news broadcasts to advise us when and where the drops would be made. The BBC messages were weird and designed to not make any sense, such as, "The oranges in Spain are bitter today." The Germans must have had a great time trying to decode that.

One evening very soon after I arrived at the *maquis* camp, there was a real flap on. The whole camp was seething with activity. A man and a woman, suspected of being French Milice, who were being held for investigation and trial, had escaped custody. They had been locked up in a room at the farm, but had managed to break out somehow. They had been given supper just a short time before the *maquis* guard noticed the breakout, so they could not have gotten too far away. Heavily armed *maquis* squads were being sent out to search for them.

The French Milice were worse than the German Gestapo, in ferreting out the Resistance Fighters, Jews and other undesirables, to please their German masters. Apparently, this couple had infiltrated the Resistance organization to such an extent that they knew most of the people and camps in the area, and if they weren't recaptured, the result could be disastrous. Even Major Knox, who normally was not affected by very much, was obviously very concerned this time.

He handed me a machine gun and suggested that we search for them in the Morlaix area. If, as the *maquis* suspected, they were French Milice, then they would undoubtedly flee to the safety of the

German Gestapo Headquarters in Morlaix, and perhaps we could intercept them. Morlaix was about a mile and a half from the camp. We were soon in position, in town, across the street from Gestapo Headquarters, where we could observe the front steps leading up to the entrance door. There were no sentries outside, so they were probably standing in the vestibule. We kept watch for hours and hours during the night, but did not see anything of the couple. I hoped that one of the *maquis* squads had found them. Just before dawn we noticed some movement in the shadows down the street.

All at once, two figures came out of the shadows and ran towards us from behind a building, and headed for the front steps of the Gestapo Headquarters. Before they could climb the steps, and before we could do anything, they were cut down by a hail of machine gun bullets fired by a *maquis* squad who, like us, had been waiting for them to appear. I took a quick look at the crumpled figures sprawled on the steps and realized that the problem with them was over. However, with all of the outside lights coming on and enemy troops moving out the door and down the steps, we had a new problem.

If the *maquis* squad, that had just killed the Milice couple, decided to engage the German troops, we would have to help them by opening up from our position, directly in front of the approaching troops. We were outnumbered, and I really hoped that the *maquis* wouldn't do their *"Vive La France"* thing this time, as it could be very costly. In my view, hit-and-run was the intelligent action here.

Looking down the street again, I was relieved to see that the squad was breaking off the engagement and moving back behind the houses. I shouted the situation to the Major and then followed him, running away from the front of the headquarters building, into the back streets, through endless backyards and lanes, to get out of town as quickly as we could. Apparently there were no *maquis* safe houses in Morlaix where we could hide out—too close to Gestapo Headquarters, no doubt.

We made it out to the farming area, but could not get back to camp because of the enemy patrol activity. We did not want to take the chance of being seen anywhere near the camp. We stayed in the bush all day and moved back to camp that night after dark.

It was a few days before they could organize another drop, but finally the BBC message was received, and we prepared to go to the "reception," as they called it, to receive the equipment dropped by the aircraft. We had arranged to arrive at the drop site with a truck to transport the heavy canisters away quickly just before the scheduled drop at 2:00 a.m. When we arrived, the signaling fires had been built, but not yet lit. We heard the aircraft overhead, the fires were lit, and the aircraft quickly came roaring in over the field, one at a time, to drop their canisters between the signal fires. I am not sure whether or not we were in radio communication with the bombers. I have a feeling that we did not even have an aldus lamp. There was really no time, since the glow from the signal fires and the roar of the bombers alerted the entire neighborhood and attracted French and Germans alike, and obviously they knew just what was going on. All we could do was to get it over with as quickly as we could and get out of the area.

In no time at all, we were knee-deep in canisters, one or two even landed on top of a signal fire and had to be quickly lifted off. After the last bomber had dropped its load and left, we loaded up the canisters into the truck with the parachutes still connected, and drove a few miles, into an empty barn, and closed the doors. We planned to unload the next day. In the meantime, it was important to get everyone out of the area just in case we had alerted the wrong people.

When we were able to retrieve the canisters and distribute them to the various camps, we found that, besides augmenting our armament with the latest weapons, the "powers that be" had finally provided the army boots we had asked for weeks before. Most of the *maquis* shoes were in tatters, as were mine. With so much walking to do, footwear had become as important as arms. Some of the *maquis* were using clogs or sabots, with a swath of hay around bare feet. After a few kilometres, they would be finished.

Because of the *maquis'* increased capability to harass the enemy, the Gestapo were stepping up their activities. Two men from the camp, one the camp barber, had been picked up as they were on their way to visit their families. Their bodies were found dumped in a field. Their heads were swollen to twice normal size, indicating their captors' desperate efforts to make them talk. Although we were sure that they had not talked, we moved camp immediately, just in case.

I was not impressed with some of the *maquis* operations, but I went along on their missions to help all I could, because although the method was questionable, the objective was not. They would wait in ambush along a highway for a German convoy to come along, usually at the top of a hill where the trucks would slow down. A young *maquis* man would run out into the middle of the highway and start firing at the lead truck, while screaming, *"Vive la France! Vive la France!"* We would commence firing from both sides of the road with everything we had, but the young fellow would invariably be killed. Being hopelessly outnumbered by the enemy now pouring out of the trucks, we would throw the last grenade and take off. Our guide's superior knowledge of the area, plus a pre-planned escape route, enabled us to get away, but it was always close. Dying in the middle of the highway like that did not seem to me to be a worthwhile goal. I always favoured making the enemy die—that left us to do something to help win.

One evening when we were moving through one of the local villages, the *maquis* told me of a wealthy French businessman who wanted to meet me. Apparently he had been collaborating with the enemy all during the war, but now realizing that Germany might not win, he wanted to, perhaps, change sides. When I met him, he offered me gifts of jams, butter, wine and Calvados to influence my opinion of him, I suppose. I refused to accept the gifts for myself, unless all of the *maquis* benefited. He accepted the conditions—my opinion of him did not change.

Following *maquis'* killing of German Occupation Troops, the Gestapo sent trucks to the local villages to pick up victims, to be taken away and shot—ten for every German killed. They selected mostly the old men from the villages, but it did not stop the *maquis* ambushes.

On July 14th, 1944, Bastille Day, the *maquis* really celebrated. I was dragged around with the major and the captain to all the camps in the area—the sergeant had to work on his codes, he said. As usual, we had to shake hands with everyone and drink endless toasts to France. The major told me that in the past he had to kiss everyone. At least I was spared that. For some reason, I could not stand the taste of the liquor. As I drank each toast, I wanted to wince and make a face but, of course, I couldn't do that. I would have insulted France, General De Gaulle, or whatever. I don't think that there was anything wrong with the liquor. They told me they had confiscated the very best from the wine cellars of the richest collaborators, having given them a compensatory chit in exchange. I doubt that the chit would ever be honoured, but who cared!

There was one reception which was somewhat different. The BBC message indicated a drop site more than fifty kilometres away—too far to walk. Four men were arriving by parachute; a Squadron Leader Smith of S.A.S. and three Frenchmen, who were to be Jedburgh team operators. They would be bringing several million in French currency to fund our operations. We planned to meet them with four Renault four-door automobiles with all the doors removed. There would be four people in each of three cars, and the fourth with driver only, to bring back the new men and the money. We were to be heavily armed so that we could shoot our way past any opposing force without the doors getting in the way. I had a 45 calibre colt automatic and a machine gun which fired 45 calibre bullets with a twenty-five-round magazine, plus two spare magazines.

We crossed the French countryside with all lights out, alternating between high speed dashes, only to have to stop and wait for the "all clear" signal provided by *maquis* scouts all along the route and back again. Although I was armed to the teeth, I never fired a shot, and I don't believe anyone else did either. It was the first *maquis* operation that I would declare successful. They were definitely improving.

I can remember being on a particularly long and tiring march with a *maquis* group, and arriving at a farm where we were to spend the rest of the night. I laid down on the hay in the barn and almost immediately fell asleep. After what seemed only minutes, I was awakened by someone shouting, *"La boche! La boche!"* I asked him how close they were, and he said something, but I couldn't catch it. I rushed outside and couldn't see anything. All at once, I could see everything. The farm was located at the top of a long sloping hill, and in the light of a bright personnel flare, I could see that the valley was crawling with enemy troops heading up the hill toward us.

They were about a mile away, but moving fast across country in a big swath. They kept firing personnel flares to light up the area in front of them. We heard later that these were 20,000 of the best fighting troops who had fought in Russia, Crete and other hot spots. They had been ordered to destroy the French Resistance in the area, once and for all. As they swept across the countryside, they ravaged farms and homes. Many people were killed and their properties burned. I gathered up my few things, my guns, and the thirty-pound generator and stand, and took off at a run down the far side of the hill, away from the approaching troops.

The farm we abandoned was in the Brest area where there are several canals and waterways. Our guide, Captain Labelle, knew the area well so that we were able to move swiftly back and forth across the lock gates. It was quite unnerving running at full speed, in almost total darkness, along the top of the narrow gates with the water thirty feet below. We walked for miles before reaching the outskirts of Brest and laid low all during the following day in some sort of unused building. We could hear the sound of a great deal of activity all around us, but we kept quiet and did not venture out. After dark, we hurried back the way we came, over the endless canal gate tops again. We rested all the next day in the bush and returned to camp the next night. While we had been on the run, another *maquis* group had captured three of the soldiers, who they suspected had been doing the killing and burning of the farms along the highway. They were sitting under a tree and were being guarded by a *maquis* fighter with a Sten gun.

One of the enemy soldiers was very young and did not seem to me to be anything more than a scared teenager. Boy! Was I wrong! He was apparently seventeen years of age, a Hitler youth, and was guilty of most of the killing. It was always left up to the *maquis* leaders to decide the fate of captured Gestapo informants. In this case, the prisoners were interrogated by Major Knox, Captain Labelle, and the *maquis* leaders, with a great number of accusers providing evidence of jewellery taken from dead women found in their pockets. I sat in the meeting and agreed with the verdict of guilty. The prisoners were ordered to dig their own graves, and afterwards, quickly shot and buried. The last I saw of the young fellow, he was being lead away with a shovel over his shoulder and a defiant look on his face. I did not question the right of these people to do this. I knew that each one had stories of one or more of their people being butchered by the enemy.

The camp was located on a high hill separated by a deep ravine from a beautiful French chateau on the next hill, which was even higher. The chateau housed a German garrison. I had been out looking around and I noticed several Germans on the roof of the chateau using binoculars to observe us and the entire countryside. They obviously had a commanding view of the area. I went inside and mentioned this to Major Knox. He was very concerned, especially since we had heard that the troops that we had just escaped from, were still searching the countryside, and it might be necessary to move in the daytime again. With the enemy watching our every move and directing the searching troops, we would not have much of a chance.

Major Knox decided to ask London to destroy it. He immediately made up an appropriate message and the sergeant sent it off. The strike was to be early the following morning, Sunday, July 30th, 1944. Saturday evening there was a big party going on at the garrison. We could hear the music and watched the German officers and their women arriving by the dozens all evening long. The party went on for hours. Finally, at about five o'clock in the morning, all was quiet. We got up early. Just after six, three R.A.F. Mosquito light bombers arrived and commenced the attack. We could see the whole thing. The aircraft bombed in turn, each taking two bombing runs across the target. Although I am not an expert in bomb size, they must have been 250- or 500-pound bombs to do the damage they did. The whole thing was over in minutes and the towering structure was reduced to rubble. I don't know just what Major Knox said in his message, but London certainly understood the urgency. There was absolutely no opposition to the bombing— either flak-wise or fighter-wise. The Germans eventually abandoned the site.

From the time I joined the *maquis,* I had been asked when the Allies would be coming to liberate them. I had always said that they would be arriving very soon, but I was beginning to wonder just what the delay was myself. General Montgomery, with the British and Canadians, was facing the main German forces at Caen and had not moved at all for about two months. As a matter of fact, the whole beachhead area had not changed in size all this time. It seemed to me that they had done nothing since I'd left the battle. I just hoped that they weren't waiting for me!

Later, I discovered that General Patton and his 3rd Army had left Dover, relying on the empty tents and the dummy camouflage to keep the Germans thinking that he was still there. In actual fact, he had embarked for the Normandy beachhead and was now ready to break out at the encircling enemy's weakest point, Avranches, with his powerful tank corp. Patton's strategy was to drive fast and hard in two directions, east towards Le Mans and west to take the great port of Brest. As Patton's tanks drove towards Brest, demolishing the enemy armour in front of them, they could not be stopped, but raced along the highway, travelling at great speed. Unfortunately, there was no immediate follow up of infantry to clean up the hundreds of thousands of enemy troops left behind who, although they had lost their heavier equipment, were far from beaten. The tanks moved so fast that refueling became a serious problem. Any force that was to supply the tanks and vehicles charging towards Brest had to be escorted by a tank force to protect it against the roving bands of enemy troops left behind.

A day or so before I left the *maquis* camp to intercept Patton's forces on the Brest highway, the straggling remnant of a company of American troops suddenly arrived in the camp. They were talking so excitedly that I had difficulty understanding them. The French-speaking *maquis* couldn't understand them at all. I finally gathered that their Infantry Company was supposed to be holding the Morlaix viaduct which was crucial to the Allied advance to Brest. They had been attacked by a superior enemy force which had killed or wounded about half of the company, including all of their officers. The remainder of the men who were not casualties, instead of rallying to drive the Germans back, broke ranks and ran away from the battle. Apparently they threw their rifles away so that they could run faster. They clustered around me, showing me snapshots of the families of their buddies who had been killed. They obviously had lost control of themselves.

I looked around at the *maquis* members, and wondered how I was going to explain this sort of action to a force that had been fighting the Germans for more than four years, and lost thousands of their friends without even considering quitting. Luckily Major Knox arrived, and since they were U.S. soldiers, and the Major's French was far superior to mine, I was able to leave it to him to explain. I suppose these troops were court-martialled, but I never heard what happened because I left the camp the next day and was caught up with my own problems.

I found out much later that the *maquis* had to do what the American troops failed to do, which was to prevent the enemy from cutting the highway to Brest by blowing up the Morlaix viaduct. After several days of furious fighting, they managed to drive the enemy away from the viaduct, but they lost a lot of their best fighting men, including Captain Labelle's brother.

Some members of the French Resistance could produce false identification papers, complete with photograph and all the necessary signatures of the French and German officials, expertly forged to look like the real thing. My papers identified me as Robér Gare, a construction worker with clearance to work in Brittany, including coastal areas. My photograph did appear to be that of an ordinary citizen, typical of the French population in the area.

I used the papers just once to get past a German roadblock soon after I joined the Resistance. I had always skirted around all such roadblocks when I travelled on my own, and I don't remember why I had to confront the enemy that time. Although I could be very aggressive in my actions, I was always against taking unnecessary risks. Unfortunately, the French character preferred the dramatic approach. They seemed to really enjoy fooling the enemy.

On this particular occasion, my Resistance guide and I were bicycling along a highway which we knew was controlled by a roadblock a short distance ahead. Since we expected to be searched, we weren't carrying any weapons. As we approached the roadblock, we slowed and then stopped in front of the two German soldiers on duty. With their automatic rifles aimed right at us, we presented our papers. I felt very uneasy and was sure that they were watching my every move as they scrutinized my papers. I wished that I had not agreed to accompany the young Resistance guide through the roadblock, as I hated to be in such a defenseless position, completely at the mercy of the enemy. I felt a little better when the soldier questioned me about my papers and I discovered that his French was worse than mine. I had been coached by my guide earlier, so that I was able to give correct answers in perfect French.

The soldiers, no doubt, assumed that I was a collaborator since I was a construction worker, and the Germans were the only ones doing any construction in France. They finally gave us back our papers, and we quickly got back on our bicycles and rode away. A long way down the highway, I looked back to see the soldiers still staring at us with their rifles raised. I don't think that they were aiming at us, but I suppose they sensed that something was wrong but weren't sure what it was. I could not relax until I was sure we were out of range of their rifles. I resolved never again to do this. In the future I would always be armed to the teeth when confronting the enemy.

25. Returning to My Base

I said good-bye to Major Knox and my *maquis* friends. As I headed out to the highway, I noticed several groups of Germans moving towards Brest in cars, trucks, motorcycles and sidecars, and even horse and wagons along the side roads and even across country, the way I had had to travel when the Germans were in charge. Now the Americans were using the highway and the Germans had to keep out of the way.

On my own again, I wanted to make sure that I joined the Americans very soon, and didn't get picked up by these enemy groups fleeing to the safety of Brest. As usual, it looked like it wasn't going to be easy, but I had no choice. Upon reaching the highway, I could see by the big gouges in the pavement that the first wave of Patton's Tank Corps had already gone through, and I wondered just how I was going to convince the Americans that I wasn't the enemy. I was really a weird sight now. I was wearing an American jacket and army boots I'd obtained from one of the drops. I had my rank on a jacket provided by the *maquis* tailor, but nothing matched. I had no idea who or what they would think I was. I seemed to have this recurring problem in France.

Suddenly, a group of six armoured cars which I had been watching a long way down the highway, came roaring around the corner. They must have been doing sixty miles per hour or better. I tried to determine if they were friend or foe, but I could not see clearly. I strained my eyes to see their markings, and finally recognized the American star and not the German cross or swastika—thank goodness. I stepped out onto the highway to flag them down. They screeched to a stop, but kept all hatches closed, and I found myself talking to a couple of machine guns which had rotated to meet me. After what seemed a very long time, a hatch opened and an officer with a two- or three-days' growth of beard and red-strained eyes asked me who I was. I told him again and he seemed satisfied. I don't think that I would have been if I'd been in charge, but he had not met the characters that I had had to deal with over the past couple of months.

He told me to climb aboard, and we roared away again towards Brest. I wanted to tell him that I had already seen Brest, and that I really wanted to go the opposite direction, but I decided against it. The crew looked exhausted. They told me that they had been driving wide open for a day and a half. They had not slept and had to continuously fight their way through the enemy forces, all the way along from Normandy.

As we drove on, I was able to observe the side of the road through a vision slot in the armour plated wall of the vehicle. I was astounded at what I saw. There were dead German soldiers all along the side of the road still sitting on motorcycles and in sidecars for a mile or more. Obviously they had been fleeing to the safety of German-held Brest, and had been overtaken by the faster moving American tank corps. They looked like toy soldiers and tinker toys. None had had time to get off their motorcycles, but had desperately tried to take cover behind houses or barns, but had not made it. It was an eerie site. The pursuing tank gunners must have had heavy trigger fingers. It appeared to be a terrible waste, and I suppose all war is a waste, but knuckling under to a tyrant like Hitler is infinitely worse.

We finally arrived at a village about twenty miles from Brest and disembarked. I was introduced to the colonel in charge, and he told me that he expected to capture Brest within a day or so. That seemed rather optimistic to me, since the Resistance had told me that the Germans had at least a half million troops in Brest with another few hundred thousand from all parts of Brittany trying to flee there. In fact, it was only after I returned to Canada that Brest finally fell. We concluded our conversation while taking cover in the ditch as enemy shells began landing nearby. German artillery, probably 88s, were firing from Brest.

I spent the night in an American M.A.S.H. hospital unit. I had to leave my Colt 45 automatic outside, as no arms were allowed. The unit was a giant tent structure. The doctors seemed very competent, and the patients were both American and German in about equal numbers. In the middle of the night, a German sniper began firing at the unit. I could hear the bullets going through the tent walls. I knew it was a German gun because the shots were from an automatic rifle—our rifles were single shot. I got up to get my Colt for some protection, but I could hear shouting and men running. The sniper, for some weird reason, was still firing, even though he must have known that he was also firing on his own people. Very soon there were several single shots, and the automatic firing stopped.

In the morning I walked over to see the colonel and he told me that an armed convoy transporting enemy prisoners would be leaving for Normandy early that afternoon. They were short of relief drivers for the thirty trucks, and he asked me to take the job. It sounded good to me. It wasn't exactly in my line, but beggars can't be choosers, they say. I thanked the colonel, wished him success in taking Brest, and rushed over to where the convoy was being formed. Besides the trucks carrying the prisoners, there were provision trucks and fuel tankers. Because of the thousands of enemy troops still very active between Brest and Normandy, a tank was put at the head of the convoy, one in the middle and one at the rear. The plan was for the head tank to engage the attacking enemy while the convoy moved on. The middle tank would take over the lead, the rear tank would move up to the middle, and the tank engaging the enemy would break off the battle and bring up the rear. My job was to be relief driver to a sergeant from Dallas, Texas. He seemed a good type except for his typical Texan accent, which was really strong.

The truck was a real monster, very high off the ground and with a three-foot steering wheel. The back of the truck was open and the prisoners, about seventy of them, were already aboard. I climbed up into the passenger's seat beside the sergeant, and the convoy, with the front tank leading, took off down the highway to Normandy. We travelled all afternoon and evening. As we passed through the towns and villages, the French citizens would first cheer and give us flowers and then jeer and scream at the prisoners as they went by. Some towns put up American flags, as if they were completely liberated. This was far from the case, as there were many German fighting units around, who were not at all willing to accept defeat. Many Germans came back and took it out on those who thought it was safe. The clean-up troops were coming, but were a week or more away. We tried to explain this to them in order to get them to remain quiet for at least a week, but they did not appear to be listening.

I was enjoying the trip so far, but probably should have gotten some sleep. I had forgotten that I was the relief driver, and when the sergeant asked me if I was ready to drive, I said sure, and jumped into the driver's seat. The steering wheel was massive and the gear box had a million gears, but it seemed powerful enough.

The convoy moved out again. It was about eleven o'clock at night now, and very dark. We travelled with no lights, but luckily I was following a fuel tanker truck which was dragging a grounding chain, and I could follow the sparks it made on the road. We were going very fast. Turning 90° corners during daylight was not particularly a problem, but at night it was very different. I would enter a sharp corner at 60 m.p.h., and the only warning I had was the sparks from the vehicle ahead as it veered to one side. I had to fully brake, take the corner, and then go full throttle again, so I wouldn't lose my position in the convoy. We were strafed by what I judged to be a couple of Junker 88 night fighters. Instead of attacking at 90° as I'd learned to do on my bombing missions, they attacked along the length of the convoy and hit nothing.

Later on, we were fired upon by enemy artillery from a hill to the left of the highway. The lead tank engaged and we all moved forward according to plan. Two of the trucks had been hit and were burning, as I drove around them. There was some delay, but fairly soon we were again moving at high speed. The two trucks had to be abandoned. None of the prisoners had been hit, no thanks to the enemy attacker. By 8:00 a.m., the sergeant was awake and the convoy stopped for a breakfast of American Army "C" rations. The prisoners were given "C" rations also. I tried to talk to a few of them, but they were not at all convinced that Germany had lost the war. Hitler was indeed an evil genius convincing great numbers of his people to think like him.

26. Going Home!

In the afternoon, we pulled into the Normandy beachhead. I left the sergeant to deliver the prisoners to the enclosure, and I reported to General Eisenhower's headquarters. They gave me authorization to travel, via hospital plane, to England, where I was to report to Air Ministry in London for debriefing.

I took time to visit my squadron, which was now based in France and flying Typhoons. I had a great talk with my C.O. and all the pilots. Our group captain, the same chap who was shot down in the North Sea earlier, was very interested in my experiences. I spent a lot of time with him. He and I seemed to have the same interest in using strategy to win this war, rather than brute strength. We talked for so long that it was too late to catch the plane to the U.K. I stayed the night with the squadron, and the next morning flew to London.

Debriefing was going to take a few days, so I decided to walk around London and see how it was standing up to the bombardment. The V1 Buzz Bombs were still arriving about three per hour as before, and V2 Rockets, two or three per day. Even though they couldn't possibly win now, the Germans kept up the vicious attacks, killing thousands of British civilians for no good reason at all.

As I strolled along, I noticed Lyon's Corner House and decided to drop in for tea one last time. I had to line up, or queue as the British put it, and wait my turn. Frank, I, and Bill, before he bought the place, used to sit in silence and listen to the stringed quartet while we sipped tea and ate cakes or buns or whatever those things were. They were baked sans sugar, sans butter and sans just about everything that normally was in them to make them taste good. For some reason we enjoyed the musicians sawing away on *The Warsaw Concerto* or some such piece of music. Maybe it was just as far away from the sound of a roaring Mustang engine and gunfire as we could get that attracted us.

I wasn't all that impressed this time, so I left and continued my stroll. As I passed a London bobby, he called me over and asked to see my identification. I didn't have any. I explained to the policeman that I knew that I was wearing a rather unusual uniform, and that he should call the Air Commodore at Air Ministry who would clear everything up. He was extremely courteous about it but rather insisted that I go with him down to the police station, where he had his superior make the call. It was an arrest! I had evaded arrest for over two months in enemy-occupied France, only to be arrested by my country's ally. I just don't know!!

I spent two more days with Air Ministry. After the debriefing, the commodore helped me locate my trunk of belongings and I was on my way home.

I travelled to Liverpool, in northern England to sail on the *New Amsterdam* to New York City. When I arrived at dock side in preparation for boarding the *New Amsterdam,* loading was well under way. About 2,000 German prisoners of war were being marched up a gangplank leading to a lock-up on one of the lower decks, with U.S. GIs hurrying them up by continually shouting "Roust! Roust!" which was "Move Quickly!" or something like that, in German. They were to be interned for the duration of the war in a camp in one of the U.S. southern states.

I had to stand by at the foot of the main gangplank leading to an upper deck, until two dozen or so United States Army Air Corps walking casualties staggered on board. I was quite close to the men as they moved up the gangplank, and I had never seen anything like it. They walked like zombies, hanging on to the rail, staring straight ahead, and shuffling along very slowly. I was told later that they were the B-17 Flying Fortress aircrew, and that they'd experienced so much trauma on daylight bombing raids against Berlin, that they were now in permanent shock. When I was eventually able to go on board it was just about dinner time so I went directly to the dining room.

The display in the dining room was very elegant and luxurious. I sat down at a table set for six, with several plates of bread and small bowls of real butter already on the table. I just stared at the heaping piles of snow-white bread, and realized that the bread I'd been eating for the past few years had not been white at all, but a very dark grey. I ate two pieces of the beautiful bread thick with butter, before the waiter arrived to take my dinner order. The bread was so good, it tasted like angel cake with icing.

In contrast to my very stormy crossing of the Atlantic from Canada to England in January, 1942, the returning voyage in September, 1944, was made in absolutely beautiful weather and calm seas. Consequently, no one became seasick and dining in the main dining room was quite enjoyable during the entire crossing.

Midway across the Atlantic ocean, I was up on the top deck taking my usual walking exercise, when I was amazed to see several dolphins swimming alongside the big troop ship, diving in and out of the bow waves. I had not expected to see anything, except maybe an enemy submarine or two, so far from shore. The dolphins followed alongside the ship for hours. People on board crowded to the railings to watch them, but I'm sure that the dolphins were oblivious to the people, and were attracted only to the huge animal that was steaming so majestically through the water.

The crossing took about seven days. We sailed into the harbour and disembarked right in the heart of New York City. I telephoned my wife from New York and couldn't get over her Canadian accent. She kept saying "heeere," instead of "heah," the way I'd become accustomed to hearing it for the past three years.

27. My Last Flying Duty - In Canada

Because I had been an evader in enemy-occupied France, I was not allowed to fly on operations again in the European theatre of war. After returning to Canada, I was asked if I would be willing to join a squadron engaged in delivering food and other supplies to troops carrying out manoeuvres in northern Saskatchewan. The project was to be known as Eskimo Exercise. I had spent the past three months or so fighting on the ground with the *maquis,* and had not flown since I was shot down in June, and I thought that it might be a good idea to do a little flying again, before getting out of the service. Here I was volunteering again!

In any case, I was posted to a squadron based at Prince Albert in northern Saskatchewan in January, 1945. My brother Norm had done his Elementary Flying on Tiger Moths on this same base back in 1940. We flew ski-equipped, single engine Norseman Transport-style aeroplanes to drop, or land on the frozen lakes to deliver supplies as required and where required, to a ground force of troops manoeuvring up in the Lac la Ronge area of the province.

My wife was in the C.W.A.C.—Canadian Women's Auxiliary Corps—and obtained a transfer from Hamilton, Ontario to Prince Albert a few weeks later, to also serve in the Eskimo Exercise project. We rented a small apartment in town with another married couple, Mac and Missy. Even though the temperature was something like 50° below zero Fahrenheit, we rather enjoyed our stay. We particularly enjoyed horse and sleigh rides, and Mac and I would throw my wife's C.W.A.C. officer off of the straw-covered sleigh, time after time. She was a bit too officious and we wanted to bring her down to earth, both figuratively and literally.

Flying was quite enjoyable. They were not fast aeroplanes, of course, and there were no operational tactics involved, but no one tried to shoot me down either, so that it was quite relaxing.

The army contingent comprised of one company of well-trained paratroops.

Why the exercise was carried out at all, I do not really know. You would almost think that we were training for a war in the north against, I suppose, the U.S.S.R. Who knows? At the end of the exercise, they had a parachute drop and a fly-over which included one of the United States' new B-29 Heavy Bombers, soon to be used to drop the atomic bomb on Japan to force their surrender.

The war with Germany came to an end on May 8, 1945. My wife and I began planning our discharge from the respective branches of the military so that we could head back into the civilian world.

My wife, Diana, Pte. Brown D.E. W21967, in her C.W.A.C. uniform.

28. Afterthoughts

The long awaited message to Europe, transmitted via the BBC, ordering the *maquis* to rise up under the leadership of the O.S.S. Jedburgh Teams, to help fight against the enemy in France, was received as an action phrase without thought of its literal meaning. I recognized it in its French form and did not even try to translate it. I heard *"Le chapeau de Napoleon . . ."* and that was enough. The actual message, *"Le chapeau de Napoleon est-il toujours a Perros-Guirec?"* was finally translated, with a lot of help from Mary and Philippe, my niece and nephew-in-law, to *"The hat of Napoleon, is it still in Perros-Guirec?"*

Perros-Guirec is a small fishing village on the English Channel coast of France, a few kilometres north of the Lacheur farm where I had hidden for over a week after being shot down. Whether or not Napoleon's hat was still in the fishing village, or indeed ever was, was not known by anyone I knew. I concluded that this final message was no more meaningful than the previous O.S.S. transmissions, which were purposely nonsensical to confuse the enemy and keep their decoding forces guessing.

Up until my final mission, I was always able to find answers to all the operational problems I encountered over the continent, and I got the job done and returned to base safely. On my final mission, the enemy gunners stopped my engine, and as I could not stay in the air, my options were limited to crash-landing or bailing out. I had been flying at 400 m.p.h. across the railroad marshalling yards, when I was hit by a shell which insisted on sharing the same space. If I had been travelling much faster, the shell would have taken my tail off, so that I would not have been able to climb to gain height to bail out, and the aircraft would have dived directly into the ground. If I had been travelling only slightly faster, the shell would have hit the cockpit, which would have eliminated all options for escape. This meant that the fact that the shell hit my engine—

although at the time I did not appreciate it—was the best of the three possibilities, in that, it was the only one that allowed me to do something to save myself. This analysis is incomplete since a fourth option could have been that if I'd been travelling slightly slower, the shell would have passed harmlessly by in front of the propeller and missed the aircraft completely. Of course, if cows had wings, they could fly too. I never ever flew slower than 400 m.p.h. in the target area, so this option is not legitimate and illustrates why I did not favour post-mortems. It made for far too much hypothetical thinking, usually not based on factual analysis.

While I was overseas, my stepmother-in-law Mrs. Humphreys and Marie, together with Mrs. Humphreys' many sisters and their families, went to church each week and lit candles to keep me and their other serving relatives free from harm. When I was reported missing, Mr. Humphreys who rarely attended church himself, although he fully supported his wife and daughter, immediately headed for the church to light, not one, but a whole rack of candles. I would be the last to question the effect this had on my eventual survival.

While in the service, it was a requirement to be inoculated against the many diseases that plague mankind. During training, we would simply line up, baring our left arms, receive our shot from the doctor and return to duty almost immediately. When I joined the squadron, inoculations became an even more informal affair. The squadron medical officer was Maltese, educated at Oxford, and had a real understanding of medicine, particularly as it applied to aircrew problems.

He was very friendly and approachable, and although I was never sick, I spent a lot of time with him discussing the medical aspects of our flying problems. I always wanted to know the answers before I encountered the problems. However, in the case of the inoculation shots, my Maltese doctor's friendliness and informality were not really an advantage. I'd drop by his office for a quick shot, and I'd have to sit and wait while he leisurely loaded the syringe, talking to me about everything under the sun, while tapping the needle to make sure that there were no air bubbles in the liquid. All the time I'd been in the service, I'd neither feared nor disliked needle shots, but sitting and waiting like this was certainly unnerving. Finally I lost my patience and asked him if he was going to give me the shot or flick the syringe needle all afternoon. Subsequent medical appointments were more formal and we saved our chit-chat for dinner at the mess.

Although my memory of the action during the war is pretty well burnt into my brain, supportive details are sometimes less clear in my mind. I can't remember, for instance, the Daily Inspection Form I filled out every time I flew. It was Form L14, but I had to be reminded by my brother, Retired Maj. Gen. N.C. Brown. Form L14 listed all the elements of the aircraft which had to be inspected daily to make sure that everything was up to specification to ensure flying safety. The engine would be run up and checked by the engine mechanic. The airframe and all flying controls would be inspected by the airframe mechanic. The VHF radio would be tested by the radio technician. The cannons would be checked and armed by the armourer. The fuel tanks would be filled, and finally everything listed on the L14 would have to be signed by the person who had performed the duty. When all functions had been completed, the form was presented to the pilot for his signature. He could check further himself, if he was not satisfied, but once he signed, the responsibility became his.

It wasn't until recently, when I reread my CO's letter to my wife, that I realized that I had had to instruct my No. 2, Flight Lieutenant Lewis, to return to base when he became separated from me during our final mission together. I had been forced to do this more times than I care to remember in my flying career, but it was usually due to bad weather. On our last mission it was because of poor visibility due to darkness, so I simply moved to Night Ranger mode and pressed on. I would have been far better off to have aborted the mission, but there was no way that I could have known the result.

Another area where my memory appears to have failed me is remembering what I ate while I was in enemy-occupied France. I remember having a French style of porridge or boiled eggs in the morning and usually an excellent stew for supper while at the Lacheur's. While celebrating Bastille Day on July 14 with the *maquis,* they cooked a small cow. When I joined the American Forces, we ate "C" rations, but I can't recollect at all what the daily fare was in the camps. Perhaps we simply picked up some fast food from the local Le McDonald's, Le Wendy's or Le Taco Bell. What do you think? It certainly would have been nice, but I guess not, since none of these establishments existed until much later in the century. We must have utilized food that was simple and could be quickly prepared as we were on the run most of the time.

After the war, I forced myself to put my experiences behind me so that I could concentrate completely on my engineering career. Now that I have dragged out all these memories to write this book, I find that I have to take a sleeping pill every night in order to get any rest at all. I just can't get to sleep without them. I'm not thinking about being jumped by enemy aircraft or anything like that. My thoughts are very ordinary and actually boring. The odd nightmare would probably be fun as long as it wasn't recurring. Maybe in time, things will calm down.

29. Triggered Memories

Following the end of the war—the European theatre, in May, and the Asian in August of 1945—an official report of the wartime history of the O.S.S. was begun under the direction of Kermit Roosevelt. In 1948, the report was complete, but it was classified and kept in a CIA vault until it was finally declassified, almost thirty years later in February 1976.

Anthony Cave Brown had just published his book, *Bodyguard of Lies* which dealt with Allied strategies for the invasion of France on D-Day, June 6, 1944. Unfortunately, at this late date he was not able to use the vast amount of information contained in the O.S.S. report in his book. Being the author most closely involved, he was asked to edit the manuscript, and to write the introduction to the published version of the report, entitled *The Secret War Report of the O.S.S.*

The introduction was comprised, in part, of actual diary quotations of day-to-day experiences of a particular Jedburgh Team operating in Finistère, Brittany, France during July and August of 1944. Of all the many such teams working in Europe after D-Day, five teams in Finistère alone, Anthony Brown selected the Giles team—the team that I'd been with—as typical. He quoted many passages from Major Knox's daily war diary. My presence with the team was entered in the diary simply as, "We were joined about this time by a Canadian pilot, Flight Lieutenant Brown, who had been shot down over Brest and was wandering through Brittany." Anthony Brown's comment to this was, "It was all like getting onto or off a bus." His comment was, no doubt, made in response to the Major's unemotional, matter-of-fact writing style, but I agreed with the Major in that after years of encounters with the enemy in the war, no one should have gotten too excited about anything.

I was with the National Research Council in Ottawa when declassification of the report took place in 1976. I can remember one of my colleagues giving me a copy of the O.S.S. war report, and being mildly surprised at the mention of my name at such a late date, but being too busy to read it in detail. Engineering problems to do with the research and development of the Machine Vision System to provide "eyes" for the Canada Arm on the NASA space shuttle took precedent. This system would enable the removal of the human factor when moving satellites into or out of space orbit.

Now that I have the time, I find that it certainly brings back a flood of memories, long suppressed at the back of my mind. I probably should have taken time to keep in touch with the very fine people involved, but I've found life just too fast and time too short for proper communication.

I did not regret having spent the better part of five years fighting the war, particularly since I managed to survive, but I felt that there was no time to waste if I was going to compete and play a part in the future of the country. Since I was sure that there wouldn't be too much call for combat Mustang pilots, however talented, I had to quickly put this behind me and strike out in a new direction.

University of Toronto Engineering Graduation Ball. Royal York Hotel, 1950.

30. Letters

Correspondence to and from India and the home front are reproduced here, or retyped for clarity, to provide a small glance at the feelings and attitudes of the people involved as the war progressed. Unfortunately, most of the letters written are not now available. The time frame covered by the letters that are available is mainly the summer of 1943 and the winter, spring and summer of 1944. My optimism and strong belief in my abilities made me accept any and all missions, but it also made me very frustrated that winning the war was taking so long. In my letter to my wife written on June 18, 1944, the day I was shot down, I spoke of getting a thirty-day leave back to Canada. Instead, I got a sixty-day outing in northern France fighting with the *maquis,* where, if anything, life became more difficult rather than easing up with time.

My wife and my folks were hit the hardest, as they knew nothing of what had happened other than that I was missing on air operations. Although I did not like it too much, at least I knew what had happened, when it happened. Shortly after I joined Jedburgh Team Giles at the *maquis* camp, I had Major Knox and the sergeant send a wireless message to O.S.S. in England, to advise that I was safe and sound. However, the O.S.S., being the forerunners of the United States' C.I.A., was a very secretive organization and did not pass the message on to anyone, least of all to the Royal Air Force Air Ministry, so that my folks were told nothing. In my de-briefing at Air Ministry after getting out of France, I mentioned the failure of O.S.S. to pass on the message, but the Air Commodore informed me that even if they had been advised, they would not have done anything differently, as they would have considered that I had simply moved from the frying pan into the fire, as it were. He said that they took no action until I had arrived back in England.

The first letter, in chronological order, is a letter to me from my brother, who in late 1941 was on an RAF Station in northeast

England completing his O.T.U. training on bombers. He was convinced that I should do anything but come overseas. My brother's second letter was from India where he and his crew were flying their RAF Lochhead Hudson Bomber against the Japanese.

Censorship of letters written by members of the military to their folks at home was routinely done during the war, to make sure that nothing said could be used by the enemy against us. It did not seem to be consistent though. My brother's letter of late 1941, for instance, had large portions cut out on several pages. Since there was a war on, my brother wrote on both sides of each page, so that cutting out passages from page one, also removed part of page two, and so on, making his letter rather difficult to understand. In contrast, while I was stationed at RAF North Weald, I wrote a letter to my wife on RAF North Weald letterhead, complete with the station telephone number, and the letter was left intact. RAF North Weald was just a few miles north of London, and at the time our Mustang Wing and a Norwegian Spitfire Wing were based there. You wouldn't think that the censor would want this information to be shared by the enemy.

There follows a series of letters to my wife who was serving as a CWAC Medical Orderly in various military hospitals in Ontario. The first year that we were apart was unpleasant, the second year was downright annoying, but by the third year it was an extremely wrenching separation. I am sure that it was just as trying for my wife and I suppose our letters reflected this strain. For myself, my Scottish heritage of reserved and stiff-upper-lip writing style was thrown to the winds. The reader will have to overlook our rather mushy messages to each other—it was all that we had left.

My determination to do everything I could in the squadron to win the war never wavered, but as the struggle dragged on, I tried to think of any way that I could to improve our way of life. I thought that if my wife came over to England, we would both be much happier. But there was a war on, and although an overseas posting was possible for her, it was not at all easy. Her Commanding

Officer in the CWAC, Captain Armstrong, who had always supported her, appeared to be dragging her feet in getting the overseas posting, and eventually we ran out of time. I suppose Captain Armstrong was thinking more logically and less emotionally than we were, so it was probably for the best. Earlier, during a leave from my squadron, I had tried to get back home with the help of a Ferry Command Pilot whose job was to ferry aircraft to and from Canada. None of my bright ideas worked out and I just had to grit my teeth a little harder and keep flying. The Second Front was imminent, and I knew that Germany would not give up without hitting England with everything it had. In my heart, I preferred my wife to be safe in Canada when that happened.

My wife's letter to me, written on June 25, 1944, after receiving an official telegram and numerous letters advising her that I was missing on air operations, completely ignored all of these and proceeded to assume, correctly as it turned out, that I had not been killed and would be back in England before too long. The censor did not have the same faith however. He stamped "Missing on War Service" on the letter and returned it to her. My wife's strange defensive refusal to believe the obvious was probably the best way that she could have handled the situation. Before the returned letter arrived, she received another official telegram advising that I had arrived safely back in England.

In my sister's letter to my wife, she says that after hearing of my escape from France, my Dad put up the flags again and told one of the men to drop the engine into the middle of the fish pond. I hope that did not happen though as I remember the pond was filled with pretty good-sized large mouth green bass.

My brother's airgraph sent from Bombay, India while he waited to board the ship for Canada summed up the situation with, "With you home and me on my way everything in the garden is lovely."

And although his concern was appreciated, I'm not sure why the Revenue Minister would write to my wife when I went missing. Perhaps the government's greed for every dime in taxes is not a modern affliction, as apparently, even in the 1940s, they just hated to lose a potential taxpayer.

In my story, I indicated that I never really understood the significance of Napoleon's hat in the BBC radio message by the *maquis* and Jedburgh Teams, but simply joined the uprising. Correspondence from my niece in November, 1994, finally cleared it all up. Mary and her husband Philippe, visited Perros-Guirec on a 50th anniversary of events which occurred in 1944. Their postcards and photographs explained everything. Why I hadn't seen the pink rock formation called Napoleon's Hat during my sorties over the coast, I can't explain except that I was, perhaps, busy doing something other than sightseeing.

Hello Rob:

Well, how is the flying getting along? Boy, I wish that you could see me now, surrounded by the fastest and most up to date Link Trainers in the world. There is nothing that these crates cannot do. They climb like a rocket, make a noise like a tank and drive everyone crazy in no time at all. No fooling, Rob, Jack Clark, Bryers, Argo and myself are now four of the best Link Instructors on the Station. Isn't that the Pay Off. Personally I prefer Blenheims but --- it over here, so don't --- you get here to find ---.

The first lad from 23 Course Sask. was killed --- last week. His name was Sandy Neal a very good friend of Jack Clark and the guy that Norm Taylor and I tied to a bunk the morning of our Wing's Party. Boy, was he drunk. He was a heck of a good guy though, and everyone of our Course 23 sure hated to see him go. He will not be the last to go though, so we don't feel as though we have seen the last of him.

I saw Tommie Watherspoon last week and he seems to be doing O.K. He is pretty badly burned but that will soon heal and he expects to be up in a month or so.

--- censored ---

Alice wrote and said that you were figuring on getting hitched soon. Well let me know when you set the date, eh?

Do you expect to come over here or take a Navigation Course? If you have a choice don't forget to take the Navigation Course, as this place is no place for a married man—or any man for that matter. No fooling Rob you would ------. It was just about then that I heard about Sandy Neal—boy, what a country.

Did I tell you that there are 3 of us to a Blenheim? The Pilot is Captain of the crate though so we consider it as our ship. My

Observer is a P/O with Astro so we should not get lost. The good thing about the set up is that P/O or no P/O he has to obey the Captain of the Aircraft - fun and stuff.

No fooling, this "Captain of the Aircraft" means more than a bucket full of pips and gold braid. Nobody can tell you what to do as soon as you leave the ground and if you don't agree with the order you don't have to obey it.

When we had finished our first training at this Station, those of us who were joed for Link Instructors were granted 3 days leave. As I had already taken a couple of days leave to see Tommie I came back for my pay and then went off for another 3 days. Lots of fun.

I have not seen Frank yet, but expect to hear from him soon. Well lad, there are a bunch of guys waiting to do ZZ Landings on the Link so I had better quit soon. If you can find any 6-20 film send it over, eh?

Now look after Diana and for John's sake don't come over here if you can possibly help it. "Better you should break a leg". Watch for low flying etc., and thanks a million for the letter. I almost for-got it.

Jack Clark and I went down to London, horsed around and then went up to Bister where Sandy Neal was stationed. Norm Taylor and some of the lads were there and we had a swell time. Jack went to Pershore to see a friend of his in the morning and I went up to Stafford to see Margaret Christie, the girl from Edinburgh, remember? We had a grand time and I landed back at camp the next morning at 10 o'clock. My leave ended at 12 the night before so they did not like it.

Boy there are a lot of planes in the air now. I can see a Blenheim, an Oxford, a Wellington and a Moth all at once.

Well so long lad look after yourself and stay away from England. There are thousands of guys here now who would give a million to be where you are now.

So long for now, Norm

June 18, 1943

196 Brown N.J. 16839

RHP India Command

Dear Rob:

Please find enclosed your Xmas card for Xmas 1942. Guess my having the wrong number on it may have lent to the Postal authorities confusion somewhat.

By the way thanks for the airgraph May 24th—note date on letterhead—not bad eh? Guess N. Africa being in our hands has speeded up the mail eh? Good show I say! Say Rob, don't you worry about my being careful—I'm retired—but for Gosh Sake keep an eye open for yourself. It only takes one slip when there are E.A.'s around and you've had it! Those "kites" of yours are sure fast but I hear that cannon shells don't waste much time either ... Do try to be careful Rob as we are going to have such a grand time in Canada when this is over. *Note—the first guy to get the V.C.—1940 is now a F/SGT—grounded—forgotten already!*

By the way, International B. Machines have really been sending me some grand letters. One even had a $570.00 gratuity in it. What this outfit needs is more mail of that nature, I say!

Your telegram arrived on schedule Rob. Think I thanked you prior to this but thanks a million again just to be sure!

Guess I told you about my leave? Well I'll just enclose a cheque form the Standard "local drive" to emphasize my claims. A close look at the faint green background on this cheque will show you what I mean.

Well, cheerio Rob—letter getting heavy so must *"aste-aste"* (go slow in Hindi).

Thanks a million for hitting the mail so often; will try to keep pace or better! Remember Diana and do be careful. Heaps of luck, Rob!

Norm

Written on RAF letterhead

Royal Air Force Station,
North Weald, Essex
January 27, 1944

Hello my Sweetheart:

How are you my little wife? Thanks a lot for the Air Graph. I had a pretty fair Christmas and New Years Di, but if you were over here it would have really been a good one. Do you really think that you can come over though Di? I wish I knew just how long this War is going to last. I am afraid that it will be another year though. I don't know if you can stand another year or not but I don't feel as if I can. Three years, my gosh! However if it has to be I can stand it alright. But if you can come over please do darling. Then again it is going to be a hard battle when the Second Front does open and in a way I would sooner have you safe in Canada when that happens. Germany still has some pretty hard punches to deliver I am afraid. I can't of course tell you much about it but I think there will be even yet a lot more civilians killed before Germany is driven to her knees. Let me know if there is a chance of you coming over and if not then just give up the idea and I will try my hardest to finish my second tour and get back to you sometime in the summer. (I hope.) Your present still hasn't arrived from India, darling, but it should be here soon.

Try to send some snapshots of yourself over though darling. I haven't had any taken for a long while now as I haven't a camera, but I will try to borrow one. This Station is quite close to London you know Di. Now if you were stationed in London, wouldn't we have a rare time. I could stay with you every night and come out to the Base in the morning. You see what you are missing by not coming over here now, Di? A cousin of one of the boys in my Squadron has a nice little apartment in London. It would suit you and I just perfectly. She said that she would lend it to us when you come over, too. She actually lives outside of London and only uses the apartment through the week. You could cook breakfast and everything, or have you forgotten how to cook by now?

Well my darling you just do what you think best and let me know soon, won't you. I don't expect to be in England after April so judge accordingly, won't you. It is too bad that you didn't see Howard though. He and I spent a day in London together just before he left for Canada. Gosh, I sure wish that I could get back even for just a week or so. Gena is expecting her baby in April isn't she, Di? You know I wish that I could send wee Arthur something, but it is hopeless over here. You can't even buy toys never mind send them out of the country. Have you seen Mr. de la Rosa lately? Well my darling I must go and get ready. I am leading two sections across this afternoon. Another hour and a half or so nearer to completing the tour and getting back to you again. Please let me know if you are able to come over. Don't come over late in the spring, what ever you do. Come over now, but after March please stay where you are, eh, sweetheart. I love you an awful lot my sweet and I need you more than life itself. I hope to see you soon my sweet.

All my love my lovely wife,

Rob

F/LT R. G. Brown,
268 Squadron, R.C.A.F. England.
Friday April 21, 1944.

Hello My Sweetheart:

How are you getting along, darling? I don't suppose you are coming over, are you Di? I think it probably would be best for you to stay in Canada now, and I will do my very best to get back later this year. We are under canvas again now. It was very cold at night at first, but it is very nice now. It really is a healthy life though. I am up at dawn every other morning. Have you received your gift yet,

Di? They are Kashmir Sapphires darling and it should look very nice on you. I sure would like to put it on your wrist myself. Well my darling the big job is very close now. I think if I can get through the worst of the Second Front, I will be eligible to go home, even if it only for a month or so. Once I get back with you I can break a leg or something to stay there. How are our savings making out darling? We had better get cracking soon or we may find ourselves with hardly anything to start out on. As soon as I get back we can start getting some kind of a plan going, eh Di? I am considering buying a camera, Di. You would like more pictures wouldn't you? I would like to take some good ones before going back to Canada. Dad said that you are sending me some really good pictures of yourself in uniform. The more you send the better, sweet. I received a very nice letter from Gena the other day. As soon as I hear that I have become an uncle for the second time I will send her some flowers. Say, you know we could have two children ourselves if this War hadn't changed things, couldn't we?

I received a letter from Mr. de la Rosa too by the way. He was talking about the T.T.C. building underground railways. Well my little wife keep writing as often as possible. Very soon I will be across the channel and I may not hear from you for months. I will be very careful my sweet. The aircraft I am flying are really first class though and if I can keep right on the top line I will be OK I am sure. I just received another Air Letter from you and you were saying that you had saved nearly $1000.00. Good work darling. I knew you could do it. I have about 150 Pounds, which is $700.00 in my account over here, so we aren't doing too badly, are we? Keep your fingers crossed Di and I will be with you at the end of this summer. I am getting lots of mail from you now darling.

All my love sweet,

Rob

F/Lt R.G.Brown,
J9451,
R.C.A.F. England.
Friday May 19, 1944.

Hello My Sweetheart:

Well my darling, it is getting pretty close to the big day now. I only hope that I will be able to get back home when the time comes for me to leave the Squadron. Gosh, it would be great to get back with you again, Di. If I do get just the one month leave, we can still have lots of fun in that time. I will have to fix it so that you get a months leave at the same time, if possible, eh darling. I am really looking forward to it. Di, you know last night after Ops, I thought that I would go to a Cinema (movie to you), in the village nearby. When I got there I discovered that some little kid show was on. I was really surprised though, Di. The name of the picture was "Lost Angel" and it was very good, so I thought anyway. You should see it and let me know what you think of it. This little girl, Margueret O'brien stars in it and although she is only six years old she really has something.

You were speaking of the socks that you knitted for me, Di. Boy, they are the only socks I have now and they are all still in good shape. There isn't a hole in any of them so far. Gosh, six months is a long time to wait to see you darling, even if I have already waited two and a half years. You know Di it is going to be really funny talking with you again. I don't know if you will have the same Canadian accent as some of the girls and boys up in R.C.A.F. Headquarters, but I really notice it now. I suppose that I have developed a bit of an English accent myself, but I just can't help laughing at the way the Canadian girls and fellows speak. We are going to have a rare time together for the first week of our leave or so. (I'll say, eh, Wow!) I haven't received your pictures yet but I am expecting them soon. You were saying in your last letter that you had finally received your bracelet and that you will have to buy a dress to go with it. Maybe

184

I didn't do the right thing, eh? Well my lovely little wife take good care of yourself and I will move Heaven and Earth to get back to see you this autumn. I love you and need you an awful lot my sweet, but as you mentioned in your last letter, it is no time to get soft. I haven't heard from Norm for a time now. I love you my wife.

All my love, sweet. (Bags more when I get back.)

Rob

F/Lt R.G.Brown,
J9451,
R.C.A.F. England.
May 26, 1944.

Hello Sweetheart:

I received your pictures today, Di. They are really swell too. I don't know how I am going to carry them when I go overseas, but I must take them with me even if I have to leave everything else behind. I am cutting down on my luggage to the bare minimum now. I figure that if I do take a lot of stuff over, then I just stand to lose a lot more. Things will happen very soon now, Di, so don't worry if you don't get a letter from me for a while. I will try to send you a cablegram every week or so, but I may not be able to do even that.

Say darling, do you have to wear your glasses all the time now? I thought that your eyes were OK now. They look very nice though, but I wouldn't wear them if you don't really have to, or you will find that you can't do without them. By the way Di, you had better forget my Squadron number etc., now and address all mail just to R.C.A.F. Overseas again. It may become a breach of security to do otherwise.

Gosh, but I wish I could see you again sweetheart. I am nearing the end of the Operational Tour now, but if the Big Show starts I am told that I must hang on in the Squadron for another few months until things stabilize. Unfortunately the more experience you have the more you will be needed. The Group Captain indicated this to me the other day and I had to reluctantly agree with him. I should still get back to you this fall though. Two of our pilots are getting married in the near future. It sure makes me envious to see them with their wives-to-be too, let me tell you. We sure are away behind now, Di, darling—two and a half years, Wow!

I am keeping a collection of "line-shoot" pictures to show you when I get back home. Some of them are pretty good too. I have a few taken over France and Belgium. If I can just last out another four or five months, I will be OK. Do you still like the Army life Di? How is Gena and the wee gaffer getting along? It is about time we had one, eh, darling? Or is it? I miss you an awful lot my little wife. We must be together soon though darling. I have just about reached the limit of my endurance. I can't imagine how you must feel, Di. It shouldn't be too long though now. I am standing-by for an Op, but at present the weather is U/S. I should be going as soon as it clears. The Bank Account is doing fine, eh, darling. Good work sweet. Well here's to this fall, darling.

All my love is for you, sweetheart,

Rob

F/Lt R.G. Brown
J9451
RCAF England
Friday June 9, 1944

Hello My Darling:

I am sorry that I couldn't send you the telegram that I expected to be able to send when the Second Front started, but it has been very difficult for us to do anything really except fly, eat and sleep. Everything is going OK with me Di. The Beachhead is established and progressing very well as you will have doubtless read in the local papers. I will soon have my tour completed now, and if I am lucky at all I should be back with you very soon. So much happens each day that a month from now seems like an eternity away. However, I am in fine shape and I can wait the extra month or so, if I have to. How is everything going, Di? I had my picture taken in London some time ago, but so far I haven't had a chance to order the finished article. I believe that a few days either side of "D" day the mail was suspended so that you may have a week or so without any mail. I have experienced this myself so I am not overly worried.

With a great deal of luck and a lot of hard work this War may be over this year. I sure do hope so. I would give anything if it could be so. In any case it won't be very long now anyway. I have a lot of stories concerning the Second Front to tell you and the folks when I come home. I can't say anything just now as it would doubtless give away a lot of important gen, so I will save them for when I get home. It certainly was a magnificent sight though, Di. I was over the Beaches that morning and what I saw really shook me. I am quite confident that we shall see victory much sooner now that the Second Front is successful. Have you heard from Norm lately, Di? I imagine that he is having a pretty busy time himself now. I am looking forward to the time when I can say farewell to England and be on my way to see you though, Di. I daren't think too much about it though, but it sure will be wonderful. If I do come over in the near future you must get a leave at the same time, eh darling. Well sweet I am going to bed early again tonight as I have to be up in the air by dawn tomorrow morning. I think of you always my sweet. I really need you Di. Take good care of yourself and keep your fingers crossed until I get back with you.

All my love darling,

Rob

F/Lt R.G. Brown,
J9451,
RCAF England,
Sunday June 18, 1944

Hello Sweetheart:

Well, my darling, here it is D+12 and I am still going strong. I will be OK now I am sure Di. Opposition is stiffening now though. I had a tussle with twelve of them a few days ago. I suppose you have heard of the "pilotless aircraft" no doubt. We call them "grumble bugs." They don't worry anyone very much except maybe keep you awake at night wondering where they are going to land. If they are Germany's only secret weapon then I think he has had it alright.

I am very close to completing my Tour now Di. I am looking forward to a trip home when I do, too. I should be able to do it, but I suppose we must just wait and see. Gosh! I would like to see you again darling. If I do get a leave we must get a car somewhere and go up North or somewhere, eh. I have an awful lot to talk to you about. We could go up to one of the northern lakes or somewhere like that. Or would you rather see some life? Whichever you prefer darling.

I am getting the pictures that I had taken in about two weeks time Di. I will send one to you just as soon as I receive them. I will no doubt be overseas very shortly so I suppose my mail will slow down accordingly. I bought a canvas bag with zipper attachments, etc., for going overseas the other day. It is quite small but can hold all the stuff that I will require, I think. I am leaving my trunk in England and just taking my very few belongings which I think will be necessary. I may lose the whole works so I am cutting down to the minimum. How are you getting along in the CWAC now darling? Do you still like the life? When I do get back you will have to show me around New York if we have time, eh sweet? However I want to be alone with you most of the time. I received a nice telegram from Norm just after the Second Front started. He is really out in the wilds I believe. I sure wish that he could get home when I do, that is if I can myself. Well sweet I am looking forward to the day when I can get my leave home. Boy, am I ever. I love you an awful lot my lovely wife. Just you wait until I get home. Oh Boy! Keep your fingers crossed for the next month or so and everything will be just perfect.

All my love,

Rob

40126 S/Ldr A.G. Mann,
No. 268 Squadron,
130 Airfield,
Royal Air Force,
Army Post Office,
20th June 1944.

Dear Mrs. Brown:

It is with the deepest regret that I am writing to you about your husband's failure to return from Sunday's operations. He was engaged in an important reconnaissance mission in connection with the invasion operations with F/Lt Lewis also of 268 Squadron.

F/Lt Lewis returned and stated that he became separated from your husband during their flight over France, but continued in wireless communication for some time. Bob, who was leading his Section, gave his companion instructions to return home and announced that he was returning also. Nothing has since been heard and he must be posted as missing.

While it is unwise to be optimistic when disappearances of this nature occur, there is a possibility that he has made a safe landing in enemy territory and is a prisoner of war. Should this be the case you would normally hear in two to three months direct from the Red Cross.

Whilst in this Squadron for the past six months, I have been constantly in contact with your husband. He has been a first class Pilot and an efficient Officer.

Bob was most popular and I would like to extend to you on behalf of his many friends and myself, our sincere sympathy at this most anxious time.

Yours sincerely,
A.G. Mann S/Ldr.

Mrs. D. Brown,
C.W.A.C. Hamilton Military Hospital,
Hamilton, Ontario.

Pte Brown D.E.,
W21967
#26 Coy. CWAC,
Admin. UCATS,
Hamilton, Ontario,
June 25, 1944.

Hello My Darling;
How are you my sweetheart? I sure hope that you are alright and I am almost sure that you are. I am sure that God will spare you and bring you home safely to me. Your Dad and I got notice saying that you were missing after air operations, but I know that God knows where you are and He will protect you and give you the strength to carry on. Marie and I went to the Church yesterday and both of us lit a candle for you. I just know that you will be back with me, you just have to my darling. I couldn't live without you. There would be nothing for me to live for. I want you and only you my darling and no one or nothing else will do. However, if it is the will of God for you not to come back to me, then I will carry on for your sake and be as good a wife as I can. I love you my darling with all the love in my heart and I need you desperately. I can trust in you my darling. I know that you will always do your best to come back to me. You have always had too much desire to live to have anything else happen.

190

Well I am writing this in pencil because I am down in the park with Ivy and Tommy. I am getting my first sun bath for this summer. Gee, it is nice here. I wish you could be here with me. Wouldn't it be swell, darling? Darling, did I tell you about the course that I was going to take? It is a Nursing Orderly course and I am on it. After Pay Parade a week ago, the C.O. called me in and told me that I was to be ready to leave the next day for Toronto. So I am in Toronto at Chorley Park Hospital taking my course. It is a four week course and when I am finished I will be a qualified Nursing Orderly. Gee, it is really swell work too darling. It is very interesting to learn all about the different ways of treating and caring for patients. I am getting to like it more than ever now.

I went back to Hamilton yesterday and spent the evening with Purcey & Conny. We went to the Carnival there and had quite a nice time. They are both so crazy that it did me the world of good to go there because they made me laugh and I felt much better. Gee, I am worried about you darling, but I keep saying to myself that you are alive and alright and soon now we will get a telegram saying that you are safe and well. Maybe darling when they find you they will bring you back to Canada and to me, eh darling. I am writing to you just the same as ever to let you know that I never lost any hope and that I still trust you and had faith that God will bring you back to me and that this is His way of bringing you home sooner. You know darling everything happens for the best. So darling keep your chin up and keep faith and we will be together real soon I am sure. Darling I know that I love you and I love you dearly with all my heart and soul and I need you more than anything in this whole world. Marie and Jack picked out their wedding ring yesterday. Ivy and Tommy are fine. Mr and Mrs Humphreys are fine and send their best luck and regards to you. Gena is up at the lake with the two kids and the Geddises. So my darling always say your prayers and trust in God to do the best for you and I. Think of me and dream of me. I will always be dreaming and thinking of you, my darling. I love you my darling and I need you always,

Di, xxxxx

Ottawa, Canada, 28th June, 1944
CWAC W21967,
Brown, D.E.,
Hamilton Military Hospital,
Hamilton, Ontario.

Dear Mrs. Brown:

It is with deep regret that I must confirm our recent telegram informing you that your husband, Flight Lieutenant Robert Gordon Brown, is reported missing on Active Service.

Advice has been received from the Royal Canadian Air Force Casualties Officer, Overseas, that your husband was the sole occupant of an aircraft which failed to return to its base after air operations over Versailles-Rambouillet, France. It is presumed that he was missing after crossing the French Coast near the Fecamp Area at 11:30 PM on June 18th, 1944.

The term "missing" is used only to indicate that his whereabouts is not immediately known and does not necessarily mean that your husband has been killed or wounded. He may have landed in enemy territory and might be a Prisoner of War. Enquiries have been made through the International Red Cross Society and all other appropriate sources and I wish to assure you that any further information received will be communicated to you immediately.

Your husband's name will not appear on the official casualty list for five weeks. You may, however, release to the Press or Radio the fact that he is reported missing, but not disclosing the date, place or his unit.

Permit me to extend to you my heartfelt sympathy during this period of uncertainty and I join with you and the members of your family in the hope that better news will be forthcoming in the near future.

Yours sincerely,
RCAF Casualty Officer,
for Chief of the Air Staff.

F/Lt R.G. Brown,
J9451,
London, England,
Sunday August 20, 1944.

Hello My Sweetheart:

I am terribly sorry that you had to go through the last two months not knowing just what had happened or how serious it was, my darling. It was very serious Di, and we can thank God that He chose to let me get away with it. For myself I could hardly hope to return to England again, but I have escaped so everything is fine. I had really thought that He had forgotten us, but He sure hasn't and we are getting everything we have hoped for, for the last three years, all in one helping. I am coming home soon darling, as I told you in my telegram. I can't say just when I will arrive, but it will be early next month, I imagine.

I will go direct to Rockcliff (near Ottawa). I will be there for perhaps one or two days and then I will get <u>one month leave.</u> I just won't be able to wait to see you again though sweet, so if I ask you to come to Ottawa for a day or so don't ask questions but come up as soon as you can. Apply at once for a month compassionate, or "passionate" (same thing isn't it?) leave, and tell them that you will give them the dates when you hear from me. I will cable you just as soon as I set foot on North America, (wherever it may be,) so that while I am travelling to Rockcliff (probably a one day trip for me,) you can fix up your leave. Get more than a month if it would make it easier. Write a letter to me at Rockcliff, (telling them to hold it there until I arrive) and let me know if you can get your leave and if you think that you can come to Ottawa. If you can't, then stay in Toronto and I will see you there. I need a lot of time to get to know you again sweet.

If you can come to Ottawa you can get a room for us in one of the Hotels and after I have finished at Rockcliff we can go on to Toronto and meet Dad and the Folks. Wow! When I reach Rockcliff and find out the gen, I will phone or wire the Chateau Laurier in Ottawa and leave a message for you, telling you when I will be able to meet you in Town, etc. You can then either be there at the appointed time or leave a message for me and a place to meet you. Rather complicated isn't it? However it should work, but if you can't make it then wire or write Rockcliff and let me know. Don't do anything until I wire you, darling. See you soon. All my love.

Rob

Department of National Defence
Ottawa, Ontario,
29th August, 1950.

Dear Flight Lieutenant Brown:

The present plans of the RCAF include an immediate requirement for a pool of trained instructors and staff pilots to be called up for active service in the event of a national emergency.

It is realized that you, as a member of the RCAF (Reserve), have not been actively engaged in Air Force flying for a considerable period and consequently, your present efficiency as a pilot may be very low. To overcome in some measure this situation and provide a maximum amount of flying training possible within limited facilities, the RCAF is introducing a Reserve Flying Programme referred to as "Chipmunk".

Under this programme a designated Royal Canadian Flying Club in the Toronto area is being equipped with a number of "Chipmunk" aircraft to provide flying practice to selected Supplementary Reserve personnel. The scope of the training will consist of twenty hours of ground and twenty hours of air training annually. To be acceptable for the training, it will be necessary for you, if you are not already a member of the Supplementary Reserve, Class "A" to transfer immediately to this component. The terms of Service for acceptance to "Chipmunk" are detailed in the attached brief.

A review of your records indicate that you are eligible for consideration for "Chipmunk" training and should you be interested in making application, you are requested to complete the attached application form and forward it to the RCAF Recruiting Officer, 55 York Street, Toronto, Ontario, post marked not later than 2359 hours, 15th September, 1950. Selections will be made on a competitive basis; the main criteria being age and previous service experience. Flying training will commence at the flying club in your locality approximately November, 1950.

It is anticipated that the response of applications from qualified personnel will greatly exceed the vacancies and, therefore, it is conceivable that although you are highly qualified for this refresher flying training you may not be selected in competition with other highly qualified candidates. Should this be the case, however, your name will be placed on the holding list for further consideration as vacancies occur at the participating flying club in your locality.

Further particulars regarding your selection or otherwise will be made known to you direct from the Recruiting Unit.

Yours truly,

(W.F. Parks)

Wing Commander, for Chief of the Air Staff.

To order more copies of

ON THE EDGE

send $19.95 plus $5.05
to cover GST, shipping and handling to:

GENERAL STORE PUBLISHING HOUSE
Box 28, 1694 Burnstown Rd.
Burnstown, Ontario
K0J 1G0

(613) 432-7697 or 1-800-465-6072
Fax 613-432-7184

URL – http://www.gsph.com.